DATE DUE

About the Author

GIRAGOS H. CHOPOURIAN was born in the city of Adana, Cilician Turkey and as a child was taken to Cyprus by his parents when the Allied Powers defaulted their responsibility and planned to pull out of conquered Turkey. He received his early education in the American Academy of Larnaca, Cyprus working his way through school. After working and teaching for nine years, he undertook graduate work at the American University of Beirut from which institution he received his B.A. degree in 1945 with honors. In the same year he received his Diploma in Religious Education from the Near East School of Theology with distinction. He did postgraduate work at several institutions: He received his Master of Religious Education degree from Andover Newton Theological School in Newton, Massachusetts; spent two years in the Harvard University Graduate School of Education doing work in Educational and Psychological Counseling; and obtained a Doctor of Philosophy degree from Temple University of Philadelphia, Pennsylvania in 1971 in Church History.

Dr. Chopourian has had 18 years of teaching experience in the American Mission High School in Cyprus and two years in the Armenian Evangelical College of Beirut, Lebanon. At the present he teaches a weekly evening course in Eastern Religions at the Georgian Court College in Lakewood, New Jersey. He served Armenian Congregational Churches in the United States for 14 years prior to being appointed Executive Secretary of the Armenian Missionary Association of America in 1969.

For a number of years Dr. Chopourian was secretary to the Staff Captain in the British Army headquartered in Larnaca during the Second World War and for a similar number of years he assisted the social service work of the Church of Scotland for the armed forces in Lebanon. He has had broad experience as teacher, preacher, traveler, writer, counselor, administrator, scout master, physical education director, youth worker. He lives with his wife in Princeton Junction, New Jersey and his three married daughters reside in the surroundings of Philadelphia.

THE
ARMENIAN EVANGELICAL
REFORMATION

The
Armenian Evangelical Reformation
CAUSES AND EFFECTS

By Giragos H. Chopourian

ARMENIAN MISSIONARY ASSOCIATION
OF AMERICA, INC., NEW YORK, 1972

To those brave souls
of the past and the future
who did stand and shall stand
for the liberty and freedom of conscience
in matters of faith and conduct

Armenag and Mariam Vartabedian

The publication cost of this book has been under-written by Mr. Benjamin Vartabedian and his wife Pam in honor of Armenag and Mariam Vartabedian, their parents. The reason for this act of devotion, apart from pursuance of the Biblical injunction to "Honor thy father and thy mother," is rooted in their parents' personality. In the first place, they were devoted Evangelicals having tasted the saving knowledge of Christ by personal experience beginning in 1905. And this book is all about the Armenian Evangelical Reformation. In the second place, they lived close to the Church of Christ, as members of the Armenian Evangelical Church of New York with Mr. Armenag Vartabedian having been voted as honorary life member, entitling him to be an exofficio member on all the Church Boards. They also made sacrifices for the Church far beyond their own means. And this book is about commitment to Christ. Finally, despite the Protestant tradition to which they belonged, they also loved and respected the Armenian Apostolic Church as true Armenians. And this book was written with the hope of bringing about a genuine ecumenical dialogue with the "Mother" Church.

Table of Contents

Foreword   xiii
Publisher's Preface   xv

I. INTRODUCTION   1

   A. *The Problem Stated*   *1*
   B. *Constantinople Armenians Envision Possibilities for Change*   *2*
   C. *Views of Armenian Authors on the Causes of Separation*   *4*
   D. *Purpose and Scope of This Study*   *6*
   E. *Fundamental Cause a Cumulative One*   *7*
   F. *The Scope and Limitations of the Study*   *8*
   G. *Two Basic Approaches to the Problem*   *9*

Part I. American Mission to Armenians

II. A SHORT SURVEY OF THE TRADITION OF THE
MISSIONARIES   13

   A. *The English Reformation Tradition*   *13*
   B. *The American Tradition*   *15*

vii

viii

    C. *Theological Discussion and the Modification of American*
          Religious Thought   18
    D. *Both Traditions Operative in the Life and Work of*
          the Missionaries   21

III. PURPOSE OF THE MISSION TO ARMENIANS   23

    A. *The Mission Objective of the American Board   23*
    B. *The Purpose of the American Board for a Mission to*
          Armenians   25
    C. *The Methods Used to Achieve the Stated Purpose   29*
    D. *Difficulties Connected with Purpose and Method   32*

IV. ATTITUDE, METHOD, AND ACTIVITIES OF THE
MISSIONARIES   35

    A. *Historic Symphonic Relationship of Church and Nation   35*
    B. *Negative Criticism of the Armenian Church   39*
    C. *Missionary Activities That Appeared Divisive   43*

Part II. The Response
of the Armenian Apostolic Church

V. A SHORT HISTORY OF REFORM TRENDS IN THE ARMENIAN
CHURCH   *51*

    A. *Conversion of Armenia and the Early Armenian Church   51*
    B. *Isolationism and Nationalization of the Armenian Church   53*

C. *Resistance Against the Established Church*   56
D. *Need for Revitalization*   58

VI. GROWING RESISTANCE AGAINST THE MISSIONARIES   62

A. *The Reign of Five Patriarchs*   62
B. *Changing Relationships*   63
C. *Causes for the Change*   66
D. *The First Round of Persecution—1839*   71
E. *Temporary Discontinuance of Persecution*   74

VII. THE FINAL SEPARATION   77

A. *The Second Round of Persecution*   77
B. *Debates and Public Discourses*   79
C. *Patriarch Choohajian's Paper of Recantation and New Creed*   81
D. *Protestant (Evangelical) Reaction*   83
E. *Excommunication Decrees*   87
F. *The Founding of the First Evangelical Church of Armenia*   91

Part III. Other Factors Aiding the Separation

VIII. THE RADICAL PROTEST OF THE REFORMED   99

A. *Persecution and the "Awakened"*   99
B. *The Nature of the Protest of the Regenerated*   103
C. *Secession the Sociological Consequence of Radical Confrontation*   105

IX. REFORM TRENDS IN TURKEY AND THE INFLUENCE OF WEST
    EUROPEAN REPRESENTATIVES IN CONSTANTINOPLE   109

    A.   *The Decline of Turkey and the Turn to the West*   *109*
    B.   *European Influence on Turkey*   *112*
    C.   *The Millet System in Turkey*   *115*
    D.   *The Establishment of the Armenian Protestant Millet*   *117*

X. CONCLUSION   124

    A.   *Secession Need Not Have Been Feared*   *124*
    B.   *Higher Clergy Acknowledge the Value of the Movement*   *126*
    C.   *What of the Future?*   *127*

APPENDIX   133

    Chronological Table   *135*
    Paper of Recantation   *136*
    The Patriarch's New Creed   *138*
    Letter of the Persecuted Christians to Patriarch Matteos
       Choohajian   *140*
    Comparison of the Theological Positions of the Two Groups   *142*
    First Anathema of the Priest Vertanes   *144*
    Second Anathema of the Armenian Patriarch,
       Anathematizing the Whole Body of Evangelical Armenians   *147*
    Declaration of Reasons for Organizing Protestant Churches   *148*
    Confession of Faith   *150*
    Williams Bay Manifesto   *152*

BIBLIOGRAPHY   157

Foreword

FOREWORD

"Controversy being permitted," wrote Milton, "falsehood will appear more false, and truth more true." F. W. Robertson, on the other hand, stated that religious controversy "destroys humble inquiry after truth, and throws all the energies into an attempt to prove ourselves right—a spirit in which no man gets at truth."

During our inquiry into the causes of the separation of the Evangelicals from the Armenian Apostolic Church, we often found ourself at either end of the pendulum prescribed by Milton and Robertson. The question is still open as to whether "the evils of controversy are transitory, while its benefits are permanent," or vice versa. One thing is certain. The physical, psychological, and sociological makeup of man is so constructed that freedom of expression needs to be guaranteed.

This work, written with a faithfulness to what might be called the doctrine of fairness, might very well be criticised by all three parties—the Armenian Apostolic, the Armenian Evangelicals, and the American Mission. We believe therein is our contribution to scholarship and to human existence.

We are eternally grateful to the many writers of the past, from whose thoughts we benefited greatly. But, first and foremost, this writer is indebted to his wife and three daughters who were extremely patient with him during his "trials and tribulations." His sincere thanks are also extended to his advisor and chairman of the Examining Committee at Temple University, Dr. F. Ernest Stoeffler, who provided wise counsel and encouragement.

Thanks are also due to the following individuals and institutions or libraries that contributed towards this research: to His Holiness Catholicos Khoren of Antelias, for making his librarian available to assist me to search material in the Seminary library in Antelias near Beirut; to his Graces, Archbishops Torkom Manoogian and Hrant Khatchadourian for their valuable cooperation; to His Beatitude Patriarch Shnorhk Kaloustian of Istanbul for an audience to discover what materials might have existed in the library of the Patriarchate; to Mr. Nazar Y. Daghlian for reading the draft to be presented to the Examining Committee and for making valuable suggestions; to the Reverend Dicran Kassouny, M. D., for writing the preface to the work and for encouraging the publication of the work by the Armenian Missionary Association of America; to Mrs. Robert McLean at Princeton for her patience and faithfulness in producing a near-perfect draft; to Mr. Puzant Yeghiayan of Antelias for making his manuscript on the Separation of the Denominations available; to the Congregational Library in Boston for the rich documents it contained pertaining to the period; to the Harvard University libraries, the library of the Andover Newton Theological School, and the library of the Mekhitarists at St. Lazarre, Venice whose abbot made his librarian available to us for a full day. Last but not least the assistance of Messrs. Set Momjian and Steven Mardiguian is appreciated greatly, the former having made numerous offset copies of the dissertation available and the latter having proof-read the printing.

C. H. Chopourian
January 31, 1972

PUBLISHER'S
PREFACE

The Armenian Evangelical Community comprises but a small fragment of our nation. It cannot be denied, however, that it has manifested a vitality and effectiveness far beyond its numerical percentage.

But on this earthly habitation, nothing is perfect and few if any blessings come unmixed: for every gain there is some loss. The Armenian Evangelical Movement is no exception.

How did it all begin? What were the underlying causes, overt and latent motives, preventable and inevitable events that finally led to the separate formation of an "Armenian Evangelical Church" ("The Evangelical Church of Armenia," more exactly) in 1846?

On the occasion of the one hundredth anniversary of this crucial happening, two major publications came out that contained a detailed account of the beginnings. One was the *Loossashavigh* (The Path of Light) by the late Reverend Yeghia S. Kassouny and the other the *Vossgemadian* (The Golden Book) by the Reverend Dicran J. Kherlopian. Both of these were in the Armenian language. The Armenian Missionary Association of America, which had sponsored the publication of the former, also published in English Leon Arpee's *A Century of Armenian Protestantism.*

Understandably, it might be contended that these and similar writings by members of the Armenian Protestant Community would reflect one side of the issue, that these would not only be in the manner of an "apologia" but might even at times be flavored with polemicism.

The other point of view, that of the "mother" Church from whom the "separation" took place, has been presented by Avedis Berberian, an eyewitness, in his *History of Armenians: Beginning with 1772 to 1860.* A recent publication, which came out as this work was going to press, is *The Separation of the Armenian Catholic and Protestant Denominations in the Nineteenth Century*, by Puzant Yeghiayan of the Armenian Catholicate of the See of Cilicia.

For his doctoral dissertation, the Reverend Giragos H. Chopourian, at the time pastor of the Armenian Martyrs' Congregational Church of Havertown ("Philadelphia"), Pa., and now since 1969 Executive Secretary of the Armenian Missionary Association of America, set himself to study this thorny subject from a purely objective, unbiased, historical approach, trying to be fair to all parties concerned—to make the utmost effort to present the facts as they appear to be.

To what extent the author has succeeded, it will be for the dispassionate reader to say. The task is a formidable one, but veritably worthwhile.

The "gap," created by the "separation," has over the years been steadily bridged over by bonds of love and patriotic fervor; by a common agony and suffering; by united efforts toward common goals. Increasingly so, as the years pass. At this period of the 125th anniversary of the Armenian Evangelical Movement we seem to feel all the closer to our historic Church of Armenia.

Do arguments ever resolve a controversy? The question is rhetorical, the answer is obviously no. If ever a controversy was stilled, it was because of the miracle of love.

The Armenian Missionary Association of America considers Rev. Dr. G. Chopourian's dissertation not only an extremely well-done historical study, but also most timely. It is our hope that its publication will engender a deeper appreciation of the events that took place one hundred and twenty-five years ago and further promote a mutual understanding among all concerned.

The Rev. Dicran Y. Kassouny, M.D.
Chairman, Publication Committee
Armenian Missionary Association of America

THE
ARMENIAN EVANGELICAL
REFORMATION

CHAPTER I

INTRODUCTION

A. *The Problem Stated*

When on June 9, 1831,[1] the Reverend William Goodell arrived in Constantinople pursuant to the instructions of the Prudential Committee of the same year,[2] the first permanent mission station for Armenians was founded by the American Board of Commissioners for Foreign Missions. It was destined to become one of the most prominent missionary stations of the Board.

Goodell was stationed in Constantinople as a result of the decision of a consultative meeting in Malta in 1829 which was attended by missionaries on the field and the visiting Secretary of the Board.[3] The consultative meeting recommended the commencement of work among Armenians, commissioning Goodell to begin said mission as soon as he had carried his Armeno-Turkish[4] version of the New Testament through the press.[5] By July 1, 1846, a small group of adherents to the teachings of the missionaries had entered into a solemn covenant and founded the First Evangelical Church of Armenia and the first Armenian Evangelical Church in Constantinople.[6]

The American Board, as well as the missionaries of the station, have stated repeatedly that they had had no intention of bringing about a separation. James L. Barton, Secretary of the American Board, is absolute and categorical in the following passage:

> In order that misunderstanding may be cleared up, it should be stated here that missionaries to the Armenians and Greeks were not sent to divide the churches or to separate out those who should accept education and read the Bible in the vernacular. Their one supreme endeavor was to help the Armenians and the Greeks work out a quiet but genuine reform in their respective churches. The missionaries made no attacks upon churches, their customs, or beliefs, but strove by positive, quiet effort to show the necessary changes.

1. *Missionary Herald*, 1831, p. 319.
2. *Ibid.*, p. 280.
3. H.G.O. Dwight, *Christianity in Turkey* (London: James Nesbit & Co., 1854), p. 31.
4. Turkish language, with Armenian characters.
5. John O. Chules and Thomas Smith, *The Origin and History of Missions* (Boston: Gould, Kendall & Lincoln, 1837), p. 309.
6. E.D.G. Prime, *Forty Years in the Turkish Empire* (New York: Robert Carter & Bros., 1883), p. 317.

... When the separation did come, it was in spite of every effort of the missionaries to prevent it.[7]

Secretary Barton continues:

> There was no desire to form among the Armenians an evangelical or Protestant Church. There was no purpose to form any organization among them, but to introduce the New Testament in the spoken tongue of the people and to assist them in working out reforms in their old Church and under their own leaders.[8]

Prime (who wrote Goodell's memoirs since the latter died soon after commencing the work) points out that the missionaries "were not actuated by any desire to gather around themselves a company of followers." He writes further that Goodell "steadily refused to baptize the children of the Greek or Armenian Christians, or to encourage members of the Greek or Armenian church to forsake in any way the communion of those churches." Finally, Prime argues that Goodell's desire was to see "the leaven of the Gospel . . . diffused among the masses of the Oriental church; to see them revived."[9]

The problem and the question therefore we pose is this: Why was a separate church created if no such intent was present? This is the burden of this research.

B. Constantinople Armenians Envision Possibilities for Change

It will be granted generally that reforms do not come about accidentally. Both in the case of reforms and revolutions, a certain amount of tension, grievances and hopes must exist before the soil can produce an event. In the case of the Reformation under Martin Luther in 1525, the American Revolution of 1776, and the French Revolution of 1789 there were elements that prepared a foundation for subsequent action. There was a great deal of dissatisfaction with the then-existing conditons; also, there were justifiable grievances against those in authority. More importantly it was a period of intellectual awakening with its moralistic, religious and humanistic drives. Finally, there was also a substantial change in the economic condition of the people—a certain amount of

---

7. James L. Barton, *Daybreak in Turkey* (Boston: The Pilgrim Press, 1908), pp. 108, 109.
8. *Ibid.*, p. 157.
9. Prime, *op. cit.*, p. 315.

progress. The combined strength of these and other factors brought on changes, reforms, revolutions.

The situation among the Armenians in Constantinople, the most enlightened city in the entire Ottoman Empire, was different from circumstances existing in the interior of Turkey where other Armenians lived, or in Armenia itself. In the ancient Metropolis there was sufficient intellectual questioning. Many had achieved a sound economic status. There were those who were in high offices in the government or were influential with the government. Constantinople was a link between declining Turkey and an advancing Europe. As a result, the eyes of many Armenians in Constantinople were opened and they envisioned possibilities for constructive changes.

Chambers confirms this openness to change when he writes that "Restless souls were found amongst the Armenians who were eager for learning, as well as for the reform of their Church."[10] Eutudjian testifies to the same truth when he says that prior to the arrival of the missionaries, there was a readiness among the Armenians for evangelical[11] truths. He remarks as follows:

> In those days there were not yet missionaries and there is no doubt that among the Armenians the minds of some were prepared to listen to the preaching of the living word of God.[12]

10. W.N. Chambers, *Yoljuluk* (London: Simpkin Marshall, Limited, 1928), p. 101.

11. The word "evangelical" appears to be used in various senses by the different parties in the struggle. Armenian Evangelicals and the American missionaries seem to imply it to mean total dependence on the Bible as the only standard, the final appeal, and the acceptable arbiter as well as "obedience only to the will of God and the instruction of the Gospel." (See, Prime, *Forty Years in the Turkish Empire*, p. 282; Eutudjian, *The Rise and Course of Evangelicalism Among Armenians*, pp. 8-11). For missionary Fisk the word implies a return to "pure," "simple," and "primitive" Christianity. (See, Annual Report, American Board, 1823, p. 118). Eutudjian believes evangelicalism means the espousing of the "orthodox" and "pure" evangelical path of the long-suffering early Armenian Church Fathers, as against the emphasis by the Armenian Church on traditions, ritual, and ceremony. (See Eutudjian, *The Rise*, etc., pp. 55, 83). Neither the Armenian Evangelicals nor the missionaries interpret the word to imply a denomination or a church organization; both parties appear to look upon it as an ideal wherein the individual Christian becomes dependent upon the power of Christ as the moving spirit in the heart—"ruled by the laws of God's word . . . according to the Scriptures." Both groups appear to make a call to go "back to the Gospel—the Evangelion." The Armenian Apostolic Church, on the other hand, appears to be interpreting the word "evangelical" to mean the adherent who refuses to recognize the sacred books of the Armenian Church Fathers in addition to the Gospel. "For this reason," writes Berberian, speaking of the evangelicals, "they called themselves evangelicals." (See Berberian, *History of Armenians*, p. 296).

12. Stepan Eutudjian, *The Rise and Course of Evangelicalism Among Armenians* (Constantinople: Arax Press, 1914), p. 46.

C. *Views of Armenian Authors on the Causes of Separation*

A number of persons have written on the Armenian Evangelical Movement and have touched upon the causes of the separation. Unfortunately, we cannot help but come to the conclusion that each one's point of view has been biased in favor of his own denominational stand. Yeghia Kassouny, who has given about fifty pages to the commencement, progress, and tensions of the Movement in his history of the Armenian Evangelical Church, assigns the basic cause to the persecuting policy of the higher Armenian clergy and Providence.[13] Dicran J. Kherlopian, writing like Kassouny on the occasion of the Golden Anniversary of the Movement, sees broad aspects of the causes but treats the subject from the Armenian Protestant point of view in the few pages he has assigned to the problem.[14] A.A. Bedikian, like the former two, argues from the evangelical point of view and points the finger at the authoritarian treatment of the newly-awakened by the Armenian Church authorities.[15] Leon Arpee, in a well-prepared and documented book, sees the roots of the awakening generally in the Armenian ethos, but assigns the awakening to the work of the missionaries strongly, seeing it as the continuation of the evangelical tradition. Regarding the "Armenianness" of the awakening he writes:

> Nor is evangelism or the preaching of the gospel, without which there can be no vital evangelism, anything new among us. We have our oldest records of it in St. Gregory. John Mandakuni would be an acceptable Protestant Preacher today. The Catholicos Moses III, in the seventeenth century, before he became a high prelate, was an outstanding modern preacher of the gospel among us. . . . Peshtimaljian, therefore, the Armenian Erasmus (neither Catholic nor Protestant), in the nineteenth century, with Dersahakian and others of his pupils, himself was only in a great succession, rather than an originator, as has been maintained, of Armenian Protestantism.[16]

Stepan Eutudjian, to whom reference has been made above, is con-

13. Yeghia Kassouny, *Loossashavigh* (Beirut: American Press, 1947).
14. Dicran J. Kherlopian, *Vossgemadian* (Beirut: Armenian Evangelical Union of the Near East, 1950).
15. A.A. Bedikian, *The Beginning of the Evangelical Movement Among Armenians* (New York: Armenian Missionary Association of America, Inc., 1964). Translated into English, entitled *The Rise of the Evangelical Movement Among Armenians* (New York: Armenian Missionary Association of America, Inc., 1970).
16. Leon Arpee, *A Century of Armenian Protestantism* (a reprint of five chapters of Leon Arpee's *The Armenian Awakening* (Chicago: The University of Chicago Press, 1909) by the Armenian Missionary Association of America, Inc. (Princeton: Princeton University Press, 1946), p. 2.

temporary to the events of the movement. He speaks for the "enlightened," considers the separation unfortunate and unnecessary, but lays the fault at the door of the persecuting policy of the higher Armenian clergy. Writing as an Apostolic, Avedis Berberian, an eyewitness, claims that the Patriarch in office attempted to convince those "trapped" by the teachings of the missionaries to return to the fold and lays the blame on the subtle methods of the sectarian missionaries. [17]

Two writers of recent years dealing with the Armenian Evangelical Movement in its relation to the Armenian Church are Nerses Paghdikian and Puzant Yeghiayan, both of the Seminary of the Antelias See in Lebanon. The former has recorded lengthily from the journals of the American missionaries as reported in the Missionary Herald. As purpose he seems to have nothing deeper or nobler than to take jibes at the missionaries when caught at undermining the grandeur of Armenians. [18] The most thorough treatment of the question is by Puzant Yeghiayan, Professor at the Antelias Seminary of the Cilician See, Lebanon, in an unpublished work in manuscript. [19] He devotes four full chapters to the Protestant denomination. He wishes, he says, to view the matter "objectively" and see the early events of the movement within "the political and missionary context." [20] Claiming that "only the Evangelical propagandist view has been presented by its apologists, whether he be missionary or Armenian," he proposes that his objective treatment of this history can restore what is missing. There is no question, however, that the point of view is biased in favor of the Armenian Church, because Evangelical sources are either discounted or ridiculed, while Armenian Apostolic Church sources are valued, praised, and shown to be historically accurate, hence reliable. The hypothesis on which Yeghiayan works is that "neither the Church of Armenia cut off and threw out its children, nor did the children wish to abandon their Mother's Home and get out," [21] but rather that the main cause of the separation was the politics of the ambassadors and courtiers of the foreign Christian nations as well as those of the missionaries. Yeghiayan believes the missionaries penetrated the more

---

17. Avedis Berberian, *History of Armenians: Beginning with 1772 to 1860* (Constantinople: Boghos Kirishjian & Co. Press, 1871).
18. Nerses Paghdikian, *The Entry of Protestantism into the World of the Dzopk.* Appeared in the periodical *Agoss* (Beirut, Lebanon, between 1955 to 1959).
19. Puzant Yeghiayan, *The Why and How of the Separation of the Armenian Denominations.* In Manuscript. (This researcher purchased all pertinent portions of the Yeghiayan manuscript in order to treat his subject in the light of modern-day criticism). Published as this work was going to press: Puzant Yeghiayan, *The Separation of the Armenian Catholic and Evangelical Denominations in the Nineteenth Century* (Antelias: Press of the Armenian Catholicate of the See of Cilicia, 1971).
20. *Ibid.*, Ch. 1. p. 3. (In published work, p. 3).
21. *Ibid.*, Ch. 1, p. 6. (In published work, p. 7).

"easily-cultivable" sector of the Armenians and exploited their piety to establish a new station for their work. These missionaries were supported by the ambassadors and courtiers of the foreign Christian nations, who after the extensive Napoleonic defeat, used pressure upon the Ottoman Empire's Supreme Porte in order to guarantee to themselves deferences from the Ottoman Government.[22] In other words, Yeghiayan sees the cause of the separation in the maneuverings of the missionaries and the politics of the foreign nations. The treatment is thoroughly critical, and well-organized, but has this unfortunate weakness in that there is no psychological, sociological, or anthropological understanding of and sympathy for the causes treated. He believes the event split the nation at a time when the nation needed unity, and considers the separation to be unforgivable.

D. Purpose and Scope of this Study

The main purpose of this study is to search and identify the fundamental causes that led the Armenian Evangelicals in Turkey to secede from the Armenian Apostolic Church within a space of fifteen years and to establish the separate Armenian Evangelical (Protestant) Church of Armenia on July 1, 1846. The justification for such a research may be summarized in the following statements:

(1) An objective and fair analysis of the reasons for separation may help remove much of the misunderstanding that exists between the Armenian Evangelicals and the Armenian Apostolic.

(2) The study may open the eyes and minds of the uninitiated to the substantial impact of the Armenian Evangelical Movement on the educational, social and intellectual life of all Armenians and its influence in reforming some aspects of the life of the Armenian Apostolic Church.

(3) An understanding of the mistakes of the past, as well as the opportunities lost, may provide valuable insights for a fuller cooperation between the two groups and for an ecumenical ministry. A study of the tensions and mistakes as well as possibilities of the period between 1831 and 1846 may provide researchers or ecumenists avenues of rapprochement for a more effective ministry to all Armenians, and, hopefully, to people all over the world among whom Armenians live.

22. *Ibid.*, p. 7. (In published work, p. 8).

E. Fundamental Cause a Cumulative One

Our study of the available sources leads us to reject the hypothesis that there was any one major cause to bring about the separation, and to establish instead the hypothesis that it was a combination of factors that led to the schism. *The central argument of this study, therefore, is that the aggressive missionary zeal, the New England theology, and the life of the missionaries, coupled with a fear-laden isolationism and strict nationalism of the Armenian Apostolic Church inherited over the centuries in self-defense, along with other factors both external and internal made a clash—and hence separation—almost inevitable from the early beginning.* THAT IS, THE CUMULATIVE EFFECT OF ALL THESE FACTORS FORM THE FUNDAMENTAL CAUSE FOR THE SEPARATION RATHER THAN ANY ONE INDIVIDUAL FACTOR. In other words, the developing missionary theology in the affluent Christian world of Europe and America; the developing reform trends in the Ottoman Empire of the nineteenth century; the intellectual enlightenment in the world at large but especially in France which under Napoleon touched upon Mediterranean shores; the historic concept of Armenian national solidarity sustained by the Church; the rights of the Armenian Apostolic Church in the Turkish Empire; the *millet*[23] policy of the Ottoman rulers; the influential presence of foreign ambassadors in Constantinople; the coming of American missionaries; the strongly pietistic outlook of the missionaries; and the push and pull, the hopes and dreams, the mistakes and constructive thrusts of human actors all combined to light the candle of evangelical Christianity in the Ottoman Empire. A spark was needed to light the path of reform. The missionaries provided that power. Without the *millet* system of the Ottoman Empire, the American missionaries would not have been able to sustain the reformed adherents as a body since such a body would not have had any civil status before the Sublime Porte, and hence no rights at all. On the other hand, the right to be called a *millet* would not have been obtainable without the assistance of foreign ambassadors, who, at this particular time, were well received by the Sublime Porte. This means that, had the Ottoman government not turned Westward for guidance and benefits at this particular period, even foreign ambassadors might have found it difficult to upset the arrangements between the government and the Armenian patriarchate. Then again, had no strict measures been taken by the Armenian higher clergy to obstruct the growth of the movement, the lines of resistance might never have been

23. Millet, a Turkish word, means a religious community (or nation) within the Ottoman Empire with a religious head as the civic leader as well. Each millet was recognized by Sultanic decree.

drawn nor the zeal of the "changed" flagged into animated obstruction or to a sense of martyrdom. But, one factor is important and fundamental and that is the decision for the establishment of a protestant mission in Turkey. Without that, it is doubtful whether reform tendencies in the Armenian Church would have taken the nature of an awakening. However, in an age when there was a worldwide missionary movement, it was just as unlikely that Turkey, which contained at that time 'blessed' Palestine, would have failed to receive the Christian concern of people awakened to the cause of Christ and the ushering in of the Kingdom of God. Further, to say that the missionaries should not have come to Turkey for work among Armenians is tantamount to saying that missionary work must never be done.

F. The Scope and Limitations of the Study

With respect to the scope and limitations of this study, it must be pointed out that it is not meant to be an exhaustive account of the Armenian Awakening, but only a careful investigation of the causes which led to separatism. The argument is developed in three parts. In order to shed light upon the role of the missionaries in creating the problem, *part one* provides a short background of their Christian faith, the purpose of the American Board in founding a mission in Constantinople, and the methods used by the leadership in the mission field. *Part two* studies the attitude of the Armenian Apostolic Church and demonstrates that the parties are on a collision course. *Part three* investigates the nature and intensity of the protest of the persons who were "awakened" or "reformed," reflects on the reform trends in Turkey, and shows how the influence of Western Government representatives in Constantinople add other factors to the separation.

Added to the first limitation stated above, is a second one which lies in the background or tradition from which the writer comes and with which, therefore, he can approach the question. He is an Armenian, investigating the response of the Armenian Church in a struggle to hold on to its national and Christian identity. Being a Protestant by faith, he is investigating the work of Protestant missionaries whose influence had brought the saving knowledge of Christ to his grandparents. The limitation consists in the possibility of his sympathizing now with one and next with the other of the parties. Then, of course, there is this one final limitation brought on by the stormy national existence the Armenian nation and the Armenian Church has had. Though there is sufficient material for an acceptable treatment of the subject under discussion, the loss of many documents due to the unfortunate massacres of the period between 1915-1918 and the Armenian Exodus of the 1921 period from Turkey make the work impossible in respect of completeness. Added to this is the truth that due to the same causes, available sources are dispersed over many parts of the world.

G. Two Basic Approaches to the Problem

It is hoped, however, that these limitations will be counter-balanced by two sound approaches suggested by Joachim Wach, which we shall adopt, namely that of sifting the material critically and placing it in its proper context without holding to the 'immanent' or 'Here is *the* truth' position; and secondly, that of understanding sympathetically, interpreting fairly and dealing justly with the materials before us. Wach's passage regarding the first approach reads as follows:

> It is easy to see that two avenues of approach are open to the student of religious phenomena, of religious attitudes, and of personalities and groups. One approach is motivated and determined by the conviction that here is the truth. It is the 'immanent' approach, used in at least half of the sources from which the sociologist, like the historian of religion in general draws. The other approach does not exclude the possibility that the statement, 'Here is *the* truth,' is valid but tries to take advantage of all material—that positively and that negatively valued by the 'insider'—to sift and examine it critically, to place it in its context (social, historical, cultural, psychological) and to interpret the phenomenon, first, in its own nature, and, second, from the background just mentioned.[24]

About the second approach, Wach recommends that the examiner must "be careful not to confuse his own ideals, his personal philosophical predilections, or the theological and metaphysical program of the group to which he subscribes with the historical, sociological, political, and religious phenomena to be evaluated. He will, when value judgements are called for, try to judge phenomena in the light of norms he considers binding on himself but always with the desire to understand sympathetically, interpret fairly, and deal justly with the various ideals and ideas to be prescribed."[25]

---

24. Joachim Wach, *Sociology of Religion* (Chicago: The University of Chicago Press, 1944), pp. 9-10.
25. *Ibid.*, pp. 287, 288.

PART ONE

AMERICAN MISSION
TO ARMENIANS

CHAPTER II

A SHORT SURVEY OF THE TRADITION OF THE MISSIONARIES

The American missionaries had a tradition of anti-episcopacy, anti-ceremonialism, and independency dating back to the England of the sixteenth century. The predecessors of those who had transmitted that tradition to America had gone through a long struggle to reform the Church of England—to purify its service, theology, discipline, and government.

A. *The English Reformation Tradition*

The Christians who desired the purifying of the church were nicknamed Puritans. They were those English Protestants who actually favored a reformation beyond that which the crown was willing to accept yet not as radical as Anabaptists. The Puritans included Presbyterians, Independents, Separatists, and Non-Separatists.

M.M. Knappen believes that Puritanism is best begun in 1524.[1] Cremeans and Haller date Puritanism even earlier. Haller says historic Puritanism was a movement begun by the successors of Chaucer's parson (c.1387)[2] while Cremeans believes that Wyclif (c.1328-1384), the founder of Lollardy, had anticipated in the fourteenth century all the major doctrines of the sixteenth century Reformation. Those early doctrines included the following: opposition to papacy; support of clerical marriages; denunciation of the principle of monasticism; insistence on the importance of spiritual religion and the unimportance of ceremonies; the call on the state to reform a corrupt church; the offer of the Bible in English for all to read. The Lollard tradition continued, according to Cremeans, until the sixteenth century without a break and contributed the "memory of a great past" with Hugh Latimer as the echo of Wyclif. This old learning and old truth, appearing as new in the sixteenth century,

---

1. M.M. Knappen, *Tudor Puritanism* (Chicago: University of Chicago Press, 1939), Ch. 1.
2. William Haller, *The Rise of Puritanism* (New York: Columbia University Press, 1938), Ch. 1.

made England more susceptible to the influence of the Continental Reformation. [3]

Religious reformers during the reign of Henry VIII (1509-1547) were divided in their support of the monarch. A number supported the royal policy because the authority of the Pope was rejected by the King, while others noted that the Supremacy of the Pope was replaced by the Supremacy of the State and so fought the Erastian[4] position that was developing. Radicals, as a result, were executed and there were two exiles during his reign.[5] But in the process some fundamental advances had been achieved with the second Henrician Exile: Opposition to religious ceremonialism, so well illustrated by Robert Barnes' "Lives of the Popes" and William Turner's "The Huntyng;" insistence on the acceptance of the biblical standards of the teaching of Christ and the early church instead of papal standards.[6]

On the death of Henry VIII and the accession of nine-year old Edward VI, the emigres returned, re-inforced by an influx of Continental reformers. For the next generation England found itself in the reformed camp—its theology, ideal of discipline, and even its church government becoming Reformed. In the spring of 1553, the Puritan party needed only time! Preachers of advanced reformation had produced a steady drift to the left; merchants, apprentices, cloth workers, yeomen had received instruction and caught that enthusiasm which made them strong supporters of the faith in later years.[7]

The accession to the throne of Mary (1553-1558) reversed the reform trend and brought about again martyrdom[8] and exile.[9]

Elizabeth I (1558-1603), who had as objective security and power,

3. Charles Davis Cremeans, *The Reception of Calvinistic Thought in England* (Urbana: University of Illinois Press, 1949), Ch. 2.

4. Thomas Erastus' view holding to the ascendancy of the State over the Church in ecclesiastical matters. In his view the civil authorities in a state which professes but one religion have the right and the duty to exercise jurisdiction in all matters whether civil or ecclesiastical, and to punish all offences.

5. M.M. Knappen, *op. cit.*, Chapters 2, 3.

6. *Ibid.*

7. *Ibid.*, Ch. 4.

8. *Ibid.*, Ch. 5. (John Hooper, one of the martyrs, said as he faced the prospect of being burned: "I have taught this truth with my tongue . . . will confirm it with my blood.").

9. Christina Garrett in her *The Marian Exiles* (Cambridge: Cambridge University Press, 1938—Reprinted 1966) lists the names of those who had self-exiled themselves to the Continent. She claims that the 1554 exiles left England as a political party and returned in 1558. Theirs was a well-planned effort to educate the youth for the ministry later in England. They returned experienced in self-government, trained in methods of propaganda, and had a political philosophy that looked askance at the prerogative of Kings. Eight church communities had been founded (Emden, Wesel, Zurich, Strassbourg, Frankfort, Basle, Geneva, Aarau); 119 students and 67 clergy had been trained, most of whom returning in 1558-59 to play their part in the Elizabethan Settlement. Two of those became members of the Privy Council.

became a huge boulder in the path of Puritanism—unavoidable, insurmountable, immovable. The religious settlement of 1559 disillusioned the hopeful Puritans who left no stone unturned to push their anti-episcopal, anti-ceremonial, and anti-erastian reform program through press, preaching, and parliament. The reformers were blocked and all the agitation came to nothing.

However, while the Queen was able to block the government of the church by the Puritans, she was unable to prohibit or stop developments in the inner life of the individual Christian or the church. The reformers had produced a spiritual literature of great inspirational value, made preaching spiritual as against witty, and presented the Bible to the public in simple English. The numbers of examplary pastors and spiritually awake individuals had increased to form something which was tantamount to a new order or brotherhood within the English church, [10] and a warm spirituality had been cultivated so that pietistic Puritanism had progressed from *doing* to *being*—piety now centering on an immediate relationship with God, mysticism, and intuitive apprehension. [11]

By the time of the death of Queen Elizabeth, the doctrine of the Church of England had become Calvinistic and Reformed and the Gospel had penetrated into the hearts of a large number of Englishmen. Non-Conformists, specifically, had arrived at the following basic conceptions: That God is sovereign; His church must be administered according to His will; this will is made manifest in Scripture; it must not be administered according to the dictates of the civil authority. [12] Much reform had come also in the discipline and government of the Church but a Geneva type of Presbyterian Church Government had not been possible to establish. The face of the Church of England had stayed "nationalistic" and "erastian."

B. The American Tradition

The period in England to 1580 was or may be termed "Tarrying for the Magistrate," when Puritans hoped for and waited for reforms to come from the head of the state. In 1582 that hope was finally relinquished as evidenced by Robert Browne (1550-1633) who advocated separation in his "A Treatise of Reformation without Tarrying." It is true that Browne later conformed and spent the last thirty years of his life in the bosom of the

---

10. William Haller, *op. cit.*, Chapters 1 and 2.
11. F. Ernest Stoeffler, *The Rise of Evangelical Pietism* (Leiden: E.J. Brill, 1965), Ch. 2.
12. Cremeans, *op. cit.*, Ch. 5.

Established Church [13] while in contrast three of his followers, namely John Copping, Elias Thacker, and William Denys were executed in 1583 for spreading Brownist opinion and propaganda. A decade later, in 1593, Henry Barrow, John Greenwood, and John Penry were hanged for Copping-Thacker type of sedition. [14]

Separatism, however, had shown signs of existence before Robert Browne's call for a church of true believers who would abandon the non-reforming church, gather together as regenerate persons, exclude the unregenerate, and covenant together. R. Tudor Jones points out that Christopher Coleman, the Cambridge Augustine friar, had become one of the leaders of London Separatism. He demonstrates, further, that there was the "privy church" in London during the Marian persecution (1553-1558) whose minister and deacon, John Rough and Cutbert Symson, witnessed to their faith with their lives. There was also the congregation which met in Plumber's Hall in London and which was "surprised" by searchers in 1567; also, the company of seventy-seven which gathered together in the house of James Tynne in the parish of St. Martin's-in-the-Fields (1568). [15] Another congregation, which was associated with the name of Richard Fitz, elected its own pastor, elder, and deacon and had a covenant as early as 1570. [16] And, south of the Thames, Bonham and Crane had set up the Wandsworth presbytery, a Separatist church, in 1572. All these Separatist churches held to a covenant, election, regenerated membership, and discipline.

In northern Nottinghamshire John Smyth and John Robinson had organized gathered churches in Gainsborough and Scrooby respectively in 1606, but were forced to emigrate to Amsterdam in 1608. Robinson took his group to Leyden where, about seven years after his "A Justification of Separation" (1610) developed a more balanced semi-separatism. Robinson's friend, Henry Jacob, founded the Independent Church at Southwark in 1616, where the same balanced semi-separatism was practiced. [17]

Such is the tradition out of which the Congregational and Puritan Churches were created in the United States, first by the settlement in Plymouth of the Scrooby Congregation of England via Leyden in 1620 and next, the settlement of the Massachusetts Bay by Puritans in 1630. [18]

13. H.M. Dexter, *The Congregationalism of the Last Three Hundred Years* (New York: Harper and Brothers, 1880), Ch. 2; Church History (Vol. IV, Dec., 1937, No. 4), pp. 289-349.
14. M.M. Knappen, *op. cit.*, Ch. 15; R.T. Jones, *op. cit.*, pp. 13-32.
15. R. Tudor Jones, *Congregationalism in England* (London: Independent Press, Ltd., 1962), pp. 13-32.
16. *Ibid.*
17. *Ibid.*
18. Williston Walker, *A History of the Congregational Churches in the United States* (In the American Church History series. New York: The Christian Literature Co., 1894), Chs. 3, 4.

Williston Walker, a prominent historian on American Congregationalism, has popularized his claim that Plymouth fashioned Puritanism into Congregationalism. [19] This view is now challenged, in that Henry Jacob is said to have influenced John Robinson to moderate his Separatism. [20] John Thomas McNeill, in this connection, believes that Robinson was ultra-Calvinist and the defender of the Synod of Dort, but was un-Calvinistic in polity, holding to the autonomy of the local church; [21] Dexter, speaking of Robinson's "Farewell Address" to the Pilgrims ready to embark for the New World, states that Robinson's guidance to the group to be experimental was in regards to polity and not doctrine. His polity was a balanced one, requesting the immigrants to be open and experimental in the matter of polity. [22] Robinson seems to have been influenced by discussions in Leyden with William Bradshaw, Robert Parker, Paul Baynes, William Ames and Henry Jacob and preserved a link with the Separatists and the Church of England. [23]

A survey of what was brought into New England doctrinally would indicate it was strict Calvinism, as formulated at the Synod of Dort (1618-19) where William Ames [24] and John Robinson had been present. In five sets of articles the Synod asserted: (1) unconditional election; (2) a limited

---

19. *Ibid.*

20. H. Shelton Smith, Robert T. Handy, and Lefferts A. Loetscher, *American Christianity* (Vol. I, New York: Charles Scribner's, 1960), pp. 82-89. These authors argue that in the year 1912 Champlin Burrage's research demonstrated that the early Congregationalists or Independents "were merely a certain type of Puritans, and not separatists from the Church of England," and that they "did not directly obtain their opinions from either Brownists or Barrowists" but from Henry Jacob. Perry Miller of Harvard University in his *Orthodoxy In Massachusetts* did not go all the way with Burrage but he did assign the Puritans the larger role in establishing the New England Tradition. In Jacob's "Principles & Foundations of Christian Religion" it was argued (1) the visible church is a particular congregation, never a diocesan or national body; (2) the church is formally gathered through mutual covenanting; (3) the church is composed of holy or regenerate believers; (4) the supreme head of the church is Jesus Christ, from whom the church has immediate and full power to order its entire life, without determination or control by any overhead body. See Champlin Burrage, *The Early English Dissenters in the Light of Recent Research,* 1550-1641 (2 Vols., Cambridge, England, 1912) I, 281.

Other Americans who have adopted the Burrage-Miller thesis are: Raymond P. Stearns, "The New England Way in Holland," *New England Quarterly,* VI (1933), 747-92; *ibid.,* *Congregationalism in the Dutch Netherlands* (Chicago, 1940); Douglas Horton, *Congregationalism: A Study in Church Polity* (London, 1952), 52-61; Verne D. Morey, "History Corrects Itself," *Bulletin of the American Congregational Association,* V (January, 1954), 9-19.

21. John T. McNeill, *The History and Character of Calvinism* (New York: Oxford University Press, 1954), Ch. 20.

22. Dexter, *op. cit.,* Ch. 7.

23. R. Tudor Jones, *op. cit.,* pp. 13-32.

24. The theologian whose books were studied in the New England educational circles until 1780.

atonement; (3) the total depravity of man; (4) the irresistibility of grace; (5) the final perseverance of saints. [25]

C. Theological Discussion and the Modification of American Religious Thought

Church polity and the assertions made above became matters of discussion in the United States for two centuries prior to the establishing of the mission station in Constantinople. During that period regulations in church polity, membership, baptism, and the sacraments were relaxed, and in doctrine, all of the assertions of the Synod of Dort were modified so that Calvin's doctrines were reconciled with the free agency of man. The climax was reached with Nathaniel Taylor's "Concio Ad Clerum" (1828) which advocated that human nature is the occasion for sin, but not its reason—that there is no sin apart from freedom. Taylor was thus assailing the traditional ideas of imputed sin and guilt.

Joseph Haroutunian and F.H. Foster have demonstrated ably that rigid Calvinism gradually declined. Important questions were raised to which diverse answers were given. Some of these were the following: (1) Are all men saved? Samuel Hopkins argued in his "The Future State of Those Who Die in Sin" that God's justice requires that He punish the sinner to protect the dignity of His Moral Government. Joseph Bellamy's "The Nature and Glory of the Gospel of Jesus Christ" spoke of the goodness and justice of God, stating that He had to provide mercy to repenters and judgement to non-repenters to protect His authority. In opposition, Charles Chauncy wrote his "Salvation for All Men . . . " (1782) and demonstrated that an infinitely benevolent God would provide a means of salvation for all, for His goodness makes the end of God the happiness of all men. (2) Is salvation of God or of man? Jonathan Mayhew, in his "Striving to Enter in the Strait Gate" (1761) made Calvinism look irrelevant and Robert Beck argued that moral living only was necessary for salvation. (3) Is sinfulness imputed? Jonathan Edwards granted that it

25. F.L. Cross, ed. *The Oxford Dictionary of the Christian Church* (London: Oxford University Press, 1958, first published in 1957, reprinted with corrections in 1958, 1961, 1963), p. 417. Definition of the five sets of articles are as follows:

(1) - God freely choosing those whom he saves and is in no way dependent, nor is his choice conditional, on any human merits.

(2) - Christ, by his death, made possible the salvation of some men only, not all.

(3) - Man is by nature, corrupt, a creature in whom the reigning principle is sin that was originally Adam's.

(4) - Man is wholly passive in the work of regeneration, and is powerless to choose, or reject, the grace that is freely given.

(5) - Man, once the subject of grace, will never fall from that state.

was not; that it was a loss of superior principle by Adam, which made the inferior principle operative. It was a matter of depravity of the heart, not imputation. He popularized this view in his New Theology with the treatise "The Great Doctrine of Original Sin." Samuel Webster, on the other hand, said that God's goodness cannot condemn children to hell, that personal sin is punished personally and that neither knowledge nor sin can be imputed. (4) Can man reform without regeneration? "Yes," argued William Hart in his "Brief Remarks on a Number of False Propositions." He accepted that man has a natural faculty by which he discerns good and evil—that he has an inborn capacity to embrace the Gospel, but wills not to. Hopkins differed, claiming that there is an imperceptible operation of the Spirit which precedes the effort to holiness. For Hopkins, means was necessary, but did not save. To Edwards, sainthood and divine excellence depended upon the relish of the heart and that human sinfulness as a scheme of salvation was in God's sovereign conditions. (5) Is man free to will? The Edwardean theology of the time continued to relate the freedom of the will to moral agency. Nathaniel Emmons considered that moral agents cannot act but only as they are acted upon by a divine operation. But, Nathaniel Taylor, who claimed to be an Edwardean, granted man "free agency, and power of choices." In this manner of discussion and disagreement, Calvinistic concepts were changed or revolutionized: unconditional election was subsumed under God's love; limited atonement was modified until it was believed that all men are saved; total depravity was shed of its sting when man was made a moral agent; irresistible grace was restated until man was made active in salvation. [26]

The American situation had other dynamic developments which had more immediate influence on the outgoing missionaries. In the article, "The American Missionary Spirit, 1828-35" it is argued that the changing economic and political patterns in the United States made the period an age of Christian benevolence, with its religious expression. The religious phase was the united endeavor aiming at the conversion of the world. The urgency of this passion was intensified by the civil commotions witnessed in several parts of the world in 1831. These were interpreted as indications that God was preparing the way for the dissemination of his word throughout the world. [27]

Among factors that brought such an outlook was the influence of the revivals under persons like T.J. Frelinghuysen among the Dutch, the Tennents among the Presbyterians, and Jonathan Edwards among the

---

26. J. Haroutunian, *Piety Versus Moralism* (New York: Henry Holt & Co., 1932); F.H. Foster, *A Genetic History of the New England Theology* (New York: Russell & Russell, 1963).
27. *Church History* (Vol. VII, June 1938, No. 2), pp. 125-137.

Congregationalists. George Whitefield helped with the introduction of the Great Awakening. The revivals created a theological temper which introduced religious discussion [28] but also division. [29] The influence of the churches grew, and the dream of making the American nation Christian led Alexis Toqueville to remark in 1830 that there was no country in the world in which the Christian religion retained a greater influence over the souls of men than in America. [30] With the Second Awakening, which commenced about 1800, the missionary spirit rose high and by 1810 one of the greater missionary societies was founded by the banding together of Andover students. [31] Samuel Hopkins' "disinterested benevolence" as presented in his "Inquiry into the Nature of True Holiness" (1773) was elaborated, which fired many to be willing to be "damned, for the greater good." Arguing in Edwardean style about holiness being reasonable as the greatest good in the universe, Hopkins made Edwards' "love of being in general" read "love as universal benevolence or friendly affection to all intelligent beings" and went so far as to say that if being cast off by God is necessary in order to secure a greater good than one's own salvation, the Christian ought to be willing to be cast off. [32]

This impulse motivated the urgency of establishing the Kingdom of God, intensified by the Millenial concept. Jonathan Edwards highlighted the millenial theology in his *A History of the Works of Redemption*. [33] In this he saw history as the whole antecedent narrative of the causes and courses of the world—history as the law in the daily lives of men but also as the tendency and manifestation of God's divine law wherein would be fulfilled the consummation of the church in time. [34] Edwards saw God at work from the fall of man, through all vicissitudes, frustrations, and obstructions by Satan, to the salvation of man in his good and great design. "God will frustrate and confound all other designs" [35] and will bring about the thousand-year rule of Christ, according to Edwards. This will be followed by the final great apostasy and then the final judgment and the blessedness of the redeemed. [36] "Therefore," he challenged, "let

28. W.S. Hudson, *Religion in America* (New York: Charles Scribner's Sons, 1965), pp. 61-82.
29. For the literature on the conflicts between the revivalist theological leaders such as James Davenport, George Whitefield and Jonathan Edwards and anti-revivalists such as Alexander Garden, Charles Chauncy and others see *The Great Awakening*, Documents Illustrating the Crisis and Its Consequences. Edited by Alan Heimert and Perry Miller. New York: The Bobbs-Merrill Company, Inc., 1967 (Second Printing), pp. 46-61.
30. W.S. Hudson, *op. cit.*, p. 130.
31. *Ibid.*, pp. 134-157.
32. Foster, *op. cit.*, Chapter 6.
33. See *The Works of President Edwards* (10 Vols.)
34. E.H. Davidson, *Jonathan Edwards: The Narrative of a Puritan Mind* (Boston: Houghton Mifflin Co., 1966), Ch. 4.
35. *The Works of President Edwards*, p. 211.
36. *Ibid.*, pp. 400 ff.

all who are in a Christless condition seriously consider these things." [37]

Joseph Bellamy's "The Millenium" (1758) emphasized the urgency of the last days and made an eloquent appeal for volunteers to hasten the victorious establishment of God's Kingdom on earth in these words:

> Hail, noble heroes! . . . Your general has sacrificed his life . . . Wherefore lay aside every weight . . . Slay every lust . . . spread the savour of divine knowledge . . . labouring to win souls for Christ . . . and enlist as volunteers under your prince, MESSIAH. [38]

D. Both Traditions Operative in the Life and Work of the Missionaries

Most of the missionaries who went to the Armenians were from Andover Theological Seminary which had been founded in 1807. It was established by "two groups of ministers and laymen in Essex County in Massachusetts," the Old Calvinists and Hopkinsian Calvinists, who "united to oppose the 'new liberalism' which had originated in Boston and at Harvard College." [39] From 1807 to 1908 the institution had had 248 of its students appointed to missions. They were not of the liberal wing, but belonged to the new theology of Hopkins and other Edwardeans— moderates. They were men who were of course aware of the existing theological differences, and must have known the Christology of Moderate Nathaniel Emmons who had no word to justify the doctrine of the personal union of the two natures of Christ in his fight against the Unitarians. Foster suggests Emmons' Christology was Nestorian essentially. [40] However, the missionaries from Andover were men who preached with passion and conviction, believing in the agency of man but trusting the Holy Spirit to bring about the regeneration. Above all, however, as our research has led us to believe, the traditions from which the missionaries had come were mostly in operation both in their life and work. Time and again the missionary literature exposes their opposition to papacy, celibacy, ceremonialism, episcopacy, monasticism and the Armenian Church's sacraments and theology. In contrast they insist upon the importance of spiritual religion, the reform of a corrupt church, the acceptance of the biblical standards of the teaching of Christ and the early

37. *Ibid.*, p. 430.
38. Alan Heimert and Perry Miller, eds., *The Great Awakening* (New York: The Bobbs-Merrill Co., Inc., 2nd Printing, 1967), "The Millenium," pp. 609-635, quotation, pp. 633 ff.
39. F.F. Goodsell, *They Lived Their Faith* (Boston: American Board of Commissioners for Foreign Missions, 1961), p. 61.
40. Emmons' Works, 1860, Vol. II, p. 745 quoted in F.H. Foster, *A Genetic History of the New England Theology* (New York: Russell & Russell, 1963), p. 345.

church, and a revivalistic kind of preaching. They also show a great deal of independency, arising out of their own tradition, without evaluating the dangers of radical independence upon the Armenian Church.

In summation the following appears to be the image of the background of the missionary who went to the Armenians in the Ottoman Empire: "Romish" ways are an abomination to him; the Bible is his final and supreme authority; he is a convinced believer in the gathered Church; he has behind him a two-century American theological thinking, and has seen discussions bring about schisms, as a result of which a good deal of his calvinism has been modified; he is fired with the urgency of bringing the kingdom of God; his intensely developed concern for the souls of men, which he believed could be won by the Gospel of Christ, has led him to genuine commitment. The humanitarian content of American life, the theological concept of disinterested benevolence, the stimulation of the millenial interpretation of the Gospel, the intellectual equipment with which he is girded, undergirded in the meantime with the history and tradition of his forefathers have made him a committed emissary whose posture seemed to say "I have the truth." But to the Armenian Church, he is a threat. For, the Armenian Church and its leaders, engrossed in their national and church conflicts, have not advanced from their Cyrillian christology and have not seen the necessity of adjusting doctrine to the movements of the times. The Armenian populace was not going to understand the missionary—neither his commitment to the Gospel, nor his concern for the souls of men. And the Armenian Church leadership, as well as the affluent Armenian or the nationalistic intellectual, was going to reject the missionary's "Here is the truth" posture and would claim that his centuries-old Church had the truth more truly!

The traditions and the psychological and theological background of the missionary appear to be full of portent for conflict.

CHAPTER III

PURPOSE OF THE
MISSION TO ARMENIANS

A. *The Mission Objective of the American Board*

The first Annual Meeting of the American Board of Commissioners for Foreign Missions met on September 5, 1810, as a result of the decision in Bradford of the General Association of Massachusetts of June 27, 1810. The General Association of the Churches had approved the request of Adoniram Judson, Jr., Samuel Mott, Jr., Samuel J. Mills, and Samuel Newell of "personally attempting a mission to the heathen." The request of the four young seminarians read as follows:

> The undersigned, members of the Divinity College, respectfully request the attention of their Rev. Fathers, convened in the General Association at Bradford, to the following *statement* and inquiries.
> They beg leave to *state*, that their minds have been long impressed with the duty and importance of personally attempting a mission to the heathen; that the impressions on their minds have induced a serious, and they trust, a prayerful consideration of the subject in its various attitudes, particularly in relation to the probable success, and the difficulties attending such an attempt: and that, after examining all the information which they can obtain, they consider themselves as devoted to this work for life, whenever God, in his providence, shall open the way. . . .
> The undersigned, feeling their youth and inexperience, look up to their fathers in the church, and respectfully solicit their advice, direction and prayers.[1]

The Annual Meeting adopted the recommendations of a special Committee established at the Bradford meeting to institute an American Board of Commissioners for Foreign Missions of nine members and a Constitution.[2] The second article of the Constitution outlined the purpose of the organization thus:

> The object of this Board is to devise, adopt, and prosecute, ways and means for propagating the gospel among those who are destitute of the knowledge of Christianity.[3]

The object, in view of the words "destitute of the knowledge of

1. *A.B.C.F.M. Annual Report* (Boston: A.B.C.F.M., 1810), pp. 9-10.
2. *Ibid.*, pp. 9-12.
3. *Ibid.*, p. 11.

Christianity," appears to be broad enough and indefinite enough as to be interpreted to apply both to the heathen as well as the nominal Christians.

At the tenth Annual Meeting we note the establishment of a Western Asia Mission, with Levi Parsons and Pliny Fisk, both of Andover Seminary, being assigned to lead a mission to Palestine and to establish a station in Jerusalem if possible. [4] The Prudential Committee provides several reasons why their "mind and heart were drawn" toward the founding of the Western Asia mission. 1. They believed Western Asia was "the scene of those great transactions and events, which involved the destinies of mankind of all ages and all nations, for time and eternity." 2. They knew that Western Asia was composed of Mohammedan countries, with many thousands of Jews, and many thousands of nominal Christians, but they believed that "the whole mingled population is in a state of deplorable ignorance and degradation,—destitute of the means of divine knowledge, and bewildered with vain imaginations and strong delusions." 3. They expressed their indebtedness to the Jews, whom they considered to be under a "curse" however, and believed that their dereliction is not to be perpetual for through the mercy of Christians they must be restored and "time seems to have arrived for this mercy to be displayed." 4. In relation to the nominal Christians, they cherished the hope that some Christians who were alive in Christ might be "roused from their slumbers, become active in doing good, and shine as lights in those darkened regions," hoping that some small part of those who bear the Christian name "would willingly and gladly receive the Bible into their houses, and do something towards imparting the heavenly treasure, as opportunities should be afforded, to the Jews, Mohammedans and Pagans." [5] In the words of an interpreter of the American Board:

> From the beginning the American Board had its eye on the Holy Land. It seemed intolerable to its founders that Christianity's birthplace should be forever in the grip of Islam, or left to exhibit a form of Christianity, ancient and entrenched, both for the most part lifeless. [6]

On December 5, 1822, three years from the departure of Parsons and Fisk in November, 1819, William Goodell and Isaac Bird were given instructions for their missionary work in Palestine. The instructions specified that they were to apply themselves in Malta, where the press was, to the acquisition of languages spoken on the shores of the Mediterranean; they were to have India as their ultimate destination with Jerusalem, according to Parsons' recommendation, as a station; also, they

4. *A.B.C.F.M. Annual Report* (Boston: A.B.C.F.M., 1819), pp. 28-30.
5. *Ibid.*
6. William E. Strong, *Story of the American Board* (Boston: The Pilgrim Press, 1910), p. 80.

were to make exploring tours to find the state of the countries around; discharge daily duties with vigor and fidelity; make the proclamation of mercy through faith in the Savior to the multitudes of perishing souls; disregard modes and forms and aim directly at the heart; press home upon the conscience the guilt of transgression, and the lost condition of the impenitent sinner.[7] "Thus you may hope," proceeded the instructions, "by a declaration of the simple truths of the Gospel, to gain attention, to impress conviction, and, by the blessing of God, to produce an entire renovation in character of some immortal beings, who shall be seals of your ministry, and the crowns of your rejoicing, in the day of the Lord Jesus."[8] They were asked to be inventors of Good things and to "discover new modes of access and the speediest and most efficacious method of bringing divine truth into contact with the conscience and the heart."[9]

This researcher would like to comment, though, that the general objective of the American Board for Western Asia will sit well neither with the Moslems nor with the established Armenian Church. The reason for this appears to be in the fact that the American Board is proposing to "propagate the gospel" among Armenians who are already Christians and seem to "accuse" by implication that they are destitute of the knowledge of Christianity. The Moslems, on the other hand, who are satisfied with their "submission" to Allah will interpret the Mission as a "Christian Crusade" against Islam.

B. The Purpose of the American Board for A Mission to Armenians

As a matter of fact, the American Missionaries discovered that preaching the Gospel to Muslims with the idea of converting them was well nigh impossible, for the government and Muslim religious authorities would punish the converts. Conversion from Islam was an impossibility under a government which rested upon a Mohammedan basis.[10] This difficulty was fully realized by the American Board which, at the conclusion of the eighteenth Annual Meeting explained:

> As to Mohametans, there is no doubt in the mind of any man acquainted with these countries, that so long as things remain in their present state, the profession of Christianity by a Mussulman will bring upon him inevitable

---

7. Missionary Herald, (Boston: A.B.C.F.M., May, 1823), pp. 141-143.
8. *Ibid.*, p. 143.
9. *Ibid.*
10. Strong, *op. cit.*, p. 223.

and immediate death. The rulers, and the people of all ranks, would act with equal zeal, and would bring down the exterminating axe with steady and inexorable vengeance.[11]

A modern writer, Hasan Basri, stated that "One embraces Islam; but one does not, cannot leave it."[12]

But there was a large area to be 'possessed for Christianity'—Palestine, Syria, Asia Minor, Arabia, Mesopotamia, Egypt, Greece, Armenia—some two million square miles, with the dominant race, Mohammedans, but with the Armenians "the most numerous" of the divided Christian sects in the Ottoman Empire and also "the most potent."[13] Therefore, the Prudential Committee of the Board in 1829 resolved to establish a mission among Armenians of Turkey in order to evangelize[14] the Armenians so as to bring about a reform in the Armenian Apostolic Church and through it to reach the non-Christians, especially the Moslem populace. So, the object of the mission, as Goodell was instructed by the Prudential Committee in 1831, was "to reach the Armenian population of the city,— an intelligent, enterprising, and wealthy part of the people, who might be expected to exert a powerful influence for good throughout the Turkish empire, when once they should embrace the truth as it is in Jesus."[15] The researchers of the American Board claimed that there was "extensive moral ruin" in Western Asia, including the Armenians, and to repair the "extensive moral ruin" discovered, the Board instructed its workers to "publish the gospel, of which the traces have become obliterated from the minds of the people."[16]

It is important to observe that the Armenians are expected to exert "influence for good throughout the Turkish Empire" once they "embrace the truth as it is in Jesus." Reports going to the American Board from the missionaries had implied that the established Church was "corrupt." All three of the earliest official missionaries were highly critical of this Church—Smith, Dwight and Goodell. Like Dwight, Goodell is reported to have been critical of the Armenian Church, of which he wrote:

> . . . like all the Oriental churches, the Armenian had become exceedingly corrupt. It was almost wholly given up to superstition and to idolatrous worship of saints, including the Virgin Mary, pictures, & c. The Armenians hold to transubstantiation, and worship the host; and, indeed,

11. *A.B.C.F.M., Annual Report*, 1827, p. 61.
12. K.W. Morgan, Ed. Islam—*The Straight Path* (New York: The Ronald Press Co., 1958). Chapter Seven, "Islamic Culture in Turkish Areas," by Hasan Basri, p. 236.
13. Strong, *op. cit.*, p. 81.
14. "Evangelize the Armenians," for the Mission, did not imply that Armenians were non-Christians being made Christian. The Mission meant to say that the Armenians would be guided by the teachings of the Gospel.
15. Prime, *op. cit.*, p. 112.
16. *A.B.C.F.M., Annual Report*, 1832, p. 153.

have adopted most of the errors of popery . . . As with all rigid formalists, the weightier matters of the law and the gospel are considered of small account compared with the punctilious performance of religious rites and ceremonies. [17]

For this reason, Goodell's dream was "the leaven of the Gospel. . . . diffused among the masses of the Oriental Churches; to see them revived." [18]

Impressions on the "corrupt" state of the Armenian Church were created by the early contacts of the missionaries. For instance, Goodell met three higher clergy between 1824 and 1825 who had, in violation of their celibate vows, moved out of the convent at Jerusalem where there had been grave internal conflicts. The former Archbishop Jacob Aga, and the former Bishops Dionysius Garabedian, and Hagop had reported on the "sunken morals of the clergy to the lowest degree of baseness and depravity." [19]

On the positive side, it was observed that the Armenians the missionaries contacted were responsive to the Scriptures and had a pious religiosity. Two of the higher clergy named above were accepted into the American Mission church in Beirut in 1827, with their wives, Maria and Susannah, being taken in as members a month later. [20] Earlier contacts by Parsons, King, Fisk, Bird and Goodell [21] of Armenian pilgrims, travelers, and priests had impressed them with their piety and responsiveness to the gospel. Therefore, on May 26, 1824, Fisk, King, Bird and Goodell, the latter two having been designated for work in Western Asia, wrote a jointly-signed letter in Beirut recommending work among Armenians. A portion of the letter reads as follows:

But our thoughts turn to with deeper interest still to the promising field, which Armenia presents, connecting with it, perhaps, Mesopotamia, and Chaldea, and the interior of Asia Minor. The Armenians are numerous in those regions, they are intelligent and enterprising, and many of them are rich merchants, who have connection with distant parts of the world. [22]

One other early event excited the attention of the American missionaries. The reference is to the "Farewell Letter" which Jonas King wrote in 1825 as he was rounding up his first three-year term on the mission field. While leaving Syria, he addressed the letter, in Arabic, to the Syrians and gave

17. Prime, *op. cit.*, pp. 126-127.
18. *Ibid.*, p. 315.
19. *A.B.C.F.M. Annual Report*, 1825, pp. 85-87; 1827, p. 43.
20. *A.B.C.F.M. Annual Report*, 1827, p. 7.
21. See Dwight, *op. cit.*, pp. 22-23; *Missionary Herald* (Boston: A.B.C.F.M., 1822), pp. 16-17; Strong, *op. cit.*, p. 82; Chules-Smith, *op. cit.*, p. 287; *A.B.C.F.M. Annual Report*, 1824.
22. *Missionary Herald*, (Boston: A.B.C.F.M., January, 1825), p. 14.

reasons why he could not be a Catholic.[23] Bishop Dionysius Garabedian, called variously Carabed, Bishop Carabed, or Signor Wortabet[24] by the missionaries, translated the letter into Armenian and sent it to some friends in Constantinople where it created quite an excitement and caused a council to be called at the Patriarchal Church consisting of all the Armenian monks, priests, bishops and patriarchs (of whom several happened to be in the capital) and the principal Armenian laymen. On ascertaining the facts of the twelve reasons King had given for his reluctance to become a Catholic, and finding the letter agreeable to Scripture, the council resolved to introduce changes. Out of this event grew the conviction to re-establish the Armenian Seminary in Constantinople which had been discontinued on account of a fire that had destroyed the building. The principal of the original as well as the re-established Seminary was Krikor Peshtimaljian, a Biblical scholar whose influence on evangelical thought was important.[25]

The early contacts we have mentioned, the adherence of the three ecclesiastics to the evangelical cause, and the response to King's "Farewell Letter" all combined to impress the missionaries on the field as well as the Board at home with the pious religiosity of the Armenians and of the possibilities of "evangelical" work among them. The impressions, of course, were the reflections and interpretations of the missionaries; perhaps aided by many factors, such as their own enthusiasm for their mission of evangelization, their hopes, their desire to encourage the Board in its plans and arrangements and outreach. The Armenians, themselves, were to give far different interpretations to these matters. We shall see later that the three converted clergy will be accused of being disgruntled men.[26]

It is to be noted carefully then that the one over-riding purpose of the missionaries of the American Board was to "publish the gospel"—to present evangelical truths.

The missionaries on the field understood their role to be just that, namely, the presentation of evangelical truths arising out of the Scriptures. "Our whole work with them," writes Goodell to Secretary Anderson on January 27, 1843, "is emphatically a Bible work. The Bible is our standard, and the Bible is our final appeal. *And it is even more necessary for us than it was for the reformers in England, because we are foreigners.*[27] Without it, we could say one thing and the priests and

23. *Missionary Herald*, 1828, pp. 141-145.
24. The more correct spelling is Vartabed, meaning preaching regular clergy or doctor.
25. *Missionary Herald*, 1827, pp. 112-113; Dwight, *op. cit.*, p. 24; Chules-Smith, *op. cit.*, p. 291.
26. Savalanyantz, *History of Jerusalem*, Vol. II (Jerusalem Convent, 18 . . .). Savalanyantz is contemporary to the events and closely associated with the Convent at Jerusalem.
27. The underlining is ours. It is important to note this leaning on the English reformation.

bishops could say another; but where would be the umpire? It would be nowhere, and all our efforts would be like 'beating the air.' "[28]

C. The Methods to Achieve the Stated Purpose

The second important consideration for the missionary was methodology—how, in what way, is this "gospel" to be "published" to a people who are mostly illiterate and among whom not one in a thousand possessed a copy of the Scriptures in a language they understood?

The answer is located in the provision of *"An improved system of education . . . to the people of the east,"* by creating "a constellation of Lancastrian[29] schools" and furnishing these with competent and trustworthy teachers.[30] They were to superintend these schools, but their appropriate employment was to be the "preaching of the gospel, and distributing the productions of the press;" because they would generally find "the school-room to be the best place for performing both of these duties."[31] The medical missionary, like the teacher-missionary, was to have a dual role. As the missionary was to be superintendent, but use the school for the propagation of the Gospel, the medical missionary was to use his skill as a means to give the Gospel. "The Committee regard your medical skill, and all your future practice," said the instructions, "only as a means of furthering the spiritual objects of the mission."[32] Though the instructions caution the missionaries to watch the method they use, yet they are encouraged not to be ecclectic for they taught that "while you take care not needlessly to offend the prejudices of the people, you will give no countenance whatever for their superstitions."[33] Thus, the instructions

---

28. Prime, *op. cit.*, p. 282.
29. Andrew Bell, a Scottish clergyman, had first originated a system of teaching at an orphanage in Madras, India. It was a monitorial system, one pupil teaching another. Joseph Lancaster (1778-1838), an English educator, on establishing his own monitorial system of schools in England in 1798, found he could not afford to hire assistants. To have students do the work of assistants, he trained pupils to teach each other. His system was non-sectarian, in contrast to Bell's, and had many new details. In his system one teacher could teach 1,000 pupils reading, writing, and arithmetic in twelve months at a cost of only seven shillings per pupil. A pupil monitor taught ten pupils. By 1811 there were 95 Lancastrian schools in England with a student body of 30,000. The first Lancastrian school in the United States was opened in New York City in 1806. After 1818, Lancaster himself founded schools in Philadelphia, Boston, and Washington and lectured on his system in those cities. (See *Collier's Encyclopedia, op. cit.*, p. 104).
30. *A.B.C.F.M. Annual Report*, 1832, pp. 152-153.
31. *Ibid.*, p. 155.
32. *Ibid.*, p. 156.
33. *Ibid.*, p. 153.

make it abundantly clear that all activities were means to one purpose, namely the presenting of "evangelical" truths because only those may prove of inestimable value at the end. About their belief in the great effectiveness of a single "evangelical" truth properly taught, the Prudential Committee wrote to the missionaries as follows:

> After years of indefatigable labor, you may have brought but a few rays of light in contact with the minds of the people at large: very few correct ideas of the gospel may they have acquired. But these few the Holy Spirit can make effectual to the producing of a general reformation. One single fundamental truth of the gospel, fully introduced into the mind, may become, in the hands of the Spirit, a life-giving principle; and that single truth, made known through a country, may prove of incalculable benefit to the country; it may revolutionize its moral sentiments.[34]

No method can be clearer, indeed. "Evangelization" is the method and that means the introduction into the mind of "fundamental truths of the Gospel." The missionaries appear to be convinced that "evangelical" truths would ultimately carry the victory because they assume that those are "absolute truths." So schools must be created, they decided, to perform that task. This conviction of the missionaries is clearly attested to in the instructions of the American Board to the missionaries that were sent to the Burman Empire in which they are told that in teaching the Gentiles it will be their business not to vehemently "declaim against their superstitions, but in meekness and gentleness of Christ, to bring them as directly as possible to the knowledge of truth. It is the *truth*, THE TRUTH AS IT IS IN JESUS, which is *mighty through* God to the pulling down of strong holds."[35] The missionaries to the Armenians, assuming similarly that the Gospel truths would prevail ultimately, considered their role to be that of sowing the Gospel messages and letting the Word be the midwife to bring about new beings.

Eli Smith had learned from the German missionaries in Shoosha[36] that it was doubtful whether enlightening the Armenian nation without drawing away any from the Armenian communion could be carried out into complete execution. He had also observed that the "enlightened" became dissatisfied and sought "spiritual food" elsewhere. Further, he had come to the realization that there was prejudice against foreign influence so that neither the missionaries alone nor the converts, who were immediately viewed as foreigners, could effect the entire reformation of the Armenian church. Therefore he came to the following conclusion:

34. *Ibid.*, p. 157.
35. *A.B.C.F.M. Annual Report*, 1812, p. 13.
36. Shoosha, a town in Persian Armenia.

The work must be done by enlightened persons rising up from the midst of the church itself; and the greater the amount of light that is diffused through the nation before it is attempted, the more sure and complete will be the result.[37]

In essence this amounts to saying that an army of the enlightened must be created who will act as "soldier evangelists" to change the entire structure and that such an army could be developed by elevating the people by a process of education by means of the press and schools. "We must commence with *elementary schools*," said Goodell and Dwight, "to say nothing now of the universally admitted fact, that impressions can be far more easily made on the mind of a child than on that of an adult, there are other strong reasons in favor of the course proposed to be pursued among the Armenians. Very few of these people comparatively, have ever been taught to read, and almost none have been taught to think."

"Now, in what way can we bestow a richer blessing on the Armenian children, and confer a greater benefit on their nation, than by putting them in possession of the juvenile literature of our own country? Translations, then, must be or suitable books prepared, and they must be made too, or prepared, in the Armenian language."[38] In 1828 the mission at Malta had ready for printing (1) The four Gospels, translated by Goodell and Bishop Dionysius; (2) Five sermons: "On the Lord's Prayer," "New Heart the Child's Best Portion," "Thy Kingdom Come," "Christ the Way to God and Heaven," "The Great Salvation;" (3) Mr. King's Letter; and (4) "Little Henry and His Beaver."[39] In 1844, alone, the printing press at Smyrna (moved there from Malta) put out in Armenian and Armeno-Turkish printing amounting to "39,000 copies, and 4,155,200 pages. The total from the beginning in the languages of the country, is 73,233,060."[40]

So, in their effort to elevate by means of education, they followed the 'Instructions' faithfully which said, *"An improved system of education must be given to the people of the east. . . . The missionary . . . must surround himself by a constellation of Lancastrian schools, as numerous as he can effectually superintend."*[41] Their school policies worked so well that the Armenian Apostolic Church was stimulated to compete, and, created "school for school" for a while and "attempted to strengthen . . . the educational ministry."[42]

In this method of presenting evangelical truths and reforming the Armenian Church from within, the missionaries claimed they had no

37. Eli Smith, *Researches,* Volume I, p. 326.
38. Chules-Smith, *op. cit.,* p. 311.
39. *Ibid.*
40. *A.B.C.F.M. Annual Report,* 1845, p. 90.
41. *A.B.C.F.M. Annual Report,* 1832, p. 153.
42. Yeghiayan, *op. cit.,* Ch. 9, p. 13. (In published work, pp. 214-215)

intention of proselytizing. Prime, writing the memoirs of Goodell, summarizes the latter's thoughts on this and says that the missionaries "were not actuated by any desire to gather around themselves a company of followers," Goodell himself steadily refusing "to baptize the children of the Greek or Armenian Churches, or to encourage members of the Greek or Armenian church to forsake in any way the communion of those churches."[43] We shall refer to this discrepancy, as we have already noticed that Goodell took in two higher clergy as members into the mission church in Beirut. The missionaries went to great lengths to argue that no proselytizing was intended. We have observed statements to that effect in the Introduction of this work. Others writing on the work of missions have stated that fact strongly. Chambers wrote:

> The idea of the missionaries was not to establish Protestantism as such, but to give the Bible in the spoken language into the hands of the people and to make provision for its careful study as far as possible by each individual; the establishment of institutions of learning, that common education might be within the reach of all for the better development of such a spirit amongst the people as would lead them to assume at the earliest possible moment the responsibility for all work that had as its aim Gospel progress.[44]

Strong argued:

> As helpers, never as antagonists, the missionaries of the American Board went to meet the Armenian people and their Church. . . . The purpose was not to proselyte the Armenians. At first, the missionaries established no schools, but sought to encourage and aid this people in starting its own schools. Likewise at first, conducting worship only for their families and other English-speaking Christians in the city. They attended services in both Gregorian and Greek churches, often taking part at the invitation of those in authority. Their evangelising efforts were thus confined to such personal interviews as they might have with those who called upon them or whom they might meet as they went here and there.[45]

D. Difficulties Connected with Purpose and Method

This researcher is willing to grant that the motives of the American Board and their missionaries were good and worthy. He is willing to grant further that they had a concern for humanity, though they expressed this

---

43. Prime, *op. cit.*, p. 315.
44. Chambers, *op. cit.*, pp. 109-110, being a quote from his 50th Anniversary Report of the American Mission given in Adana.
45. Strong, *op. cit.*, p. 92.

concern in questionable terms when they said it was "to save perishing souls!" The souls may have been in need of regeneration, but were not in a perishing state.

Trusting their motive, however, is not the same as saying that the actions taken and the methods used in the field substantiated the statements for a policy of nonproselytizing. For instance, Strong's interpretation that 'at first' they established no schools, conducted no worship services for the local populace, confined evangelizing to callers upon them, does not explain why they changed their policy later. If that were the absolutely clear and strict policy, a few problems that the missionaries met should not have led them to change it. If the help the missionaries extended were refused and the recipients said, "We don't want you," should the original policy have been changed?

Further, the statement of the missionaries that their intention was not to proselytize contradicted their plan to present "evangelical" truths to the Armenians with a view to reforming the Armenian Church, with the additional design of having the "reformed Armenian Church" evangelize Islam. Is it ever possible to indoctrinate and not proselytize? We have seen that the teaching missionary as well as the medical missionary were to use their skill primarily to inculcate the American brand of Protestant teaching to further "the spiritual objects of the mission." When one adds to this their conviction that they had the correct biblical *truth*, it is difficult to accept the process as a mere motiveless benevolent assistance.

Therefore, their purposes of presenting evangelical truths and reforming the Armenian Church; their method of elevating by education; their conviction that they had *the truth* in Jesus—all these bore the seeds of tension and conflict. The premise of the missionary appears to have been that he could give evangelical truths without challenge, considering the Armenian Church's truth to have been vulnerable and hence unable to stand the test of the Scriptures. His premise, further, seems to have been that he could enlighten minds by his own brand of education, kneaded with Scripture teaching, without being faced with the necessity of handing over the supervision of the schools to the local Armenian Community.

Yeghiayan, in suggesting that the tragedy that occurred could have been avoided and turned into a blessing, argues that the missionaries should have had the wisdom to "hand over the direction of the Curriculum, and the moral and religious instructions to the responsibility of Armenians."[46] If his remark is to the missionary on the field, it only needs to be pointed out that the instructions of the Prudential Committee on this point were clear, namely, " . . . you will grant pecuniary aid only to schools under the superintendence of yourselves, or persons having your

46. Yeghiayan, *op. cit.*, Ch. 9, p. 12. (In published work, pp. 214-215)

fullest confidence."[47] If, however, his argument is for the ears of the American Board he seems to forget that the American Board had only one supreme object—the conversion of sinful individuals to a new life in Christ—and every activity at the disposal of the missionary was only a means to fulfill that prime purpose. There could not have been a mission without that prime purpose—not at that time in human history.

There was a further assumption on the part of the missionary, and that was that his brand of pietistic Puritan Christianity would have been acceptable. He was unprepared to sympathetically understand the genuine belief and pride of the Armenian in his own brand of theology and church discipline. Way back in 451 A.D., while putting up, knowingly, a suicidal defence of faith and nation against the Persian insistence to impose Mazdaism on the Armenians, the general of the Army had given this battle cry to his soldiers: "He who had conceived that we wear our Christianity as one does his garments, now finds that he no more can divest us of it than he can of the color of our skin, and, let us hope, never will be able to the end."[48]

To sum up the argument: the American mission to the Armenians was full of real possibilities for a genuine reformation in the nation and the ultimate utilization of the awakened (reformed) populace to effect the modernization and Westernization, and hopefully evangelization, of Turkey; but, the historical orientation of the Armenian nation vis-á-vis the orientation of the Armenian Church was of such a nature as to make it quite unlikely that an "imported" brand of Christian truth, not to say doctrine, would have been accepted as better than its own "home-grown" traditional, sacerdotal, ritualistic and ceremonial Christianity which had sustained the nation and kept it looking at the "cross" instead of the Mazdian "fire" or the Muslim "crescent" for over fifteen hundred years (311-1831). The general objective of the American Board and its purposes and methods were calling for a Protestant Reformation. The Armenian Church, which had separated even from other Orthodox Churches over doctrine, could not have countenanced such a change. This was essentially at the root of the problem.

In the next chapter, we shall investigate the mistakes of the missionaries for a fuller understanding of the causes that led to separation of a number of Armenians from the Apostolic or "Mother" Church.

---

47. *A.B.C.F.M. Annual Report*, 1832, p. 153.
48. Arpee, *A History of Armenian Christianity*, pp. 149-150.

CHAPTER IV

ATTITUDE, METHOD, AND ACTIVITIES OF THE MISSIONARIES

It has been more than hinted in the immediately previous chapter that the purposes and designs of the American Board and its missionaries contained the seeds of controversy and conflict. In this chapter it will be demonstrated that their attitude, procedure, and activities did nurture those seeds.

A. Historic Symphonic Relationship of Church and Nation

Generally speaking, there is a symphonic relationship in the Orthodox tradition between church and nation. Shaw speaking of the Greek Orthodox Church explains that the church had kept the nation together through centuries of oppression and it could not tolerate therefore anything that would impair national consciousness and unity.[1] The Church, according to Shaw, had helped keep language and folklore, had supported wars of independence, and furnished martyrs to the cause. Disloyalty to the Orthodox Church was disloyalty to the nation itself, and, therefore, a convert to Protestantism was a man without a country. Any incursion upon the loyalty of a Greek to his Church was an incursion upon his patriotism.[2]

The Armenian Church,[3] similarly, had defended the nation against oppression, and had kept language, literature, and the spirit of freedom alive. It had given martyrs for these causes. Consequently, "Christian" meant Armenian and "Armenian" stood for Christian. Adanalian accepted this intimate relationship when he wrote thus:

> The Armenian nation and the Armenian Church for many centuries have united together and become identical. The nation and the Church have

1. That is why both the mission of the Episcopal Church of America and that of the American Board of Commissioners for Foreign Missions to the Greeks was resisted stiffly by Church and Government. See Denison's *A History of the Foreign Missionary Work of the Protestant Episcopal Church*, I, and Shaw's *American Contacts with the Eastern Church*.
2. P.E. Shaw, *American Contacts with the Eastern Church, 1820-1870* (Chicago: The American Society of Church History, 1937), pp. 65-85.
3. Variously named "The Armenian Apostolic," "The Armenian Gregorian," "The Armenian Orthodox" Church.

become synonymous . . . The Church as center, has become the medium for defense and leadership as well as a life-giving source both spiritually and politically.[4]

In other words, the Armenian looked to the church for salvation in political as well as religious life. The political, cultural, social and religious life of the nation was so well integrated in the minds of the people, if not in reality, that each Armenian's pulse beat as one.

It appears from the records that the American missionaries believed this church-nation symphonic relationship to be a hindrance to the witnessing of Christ. But, contrary to the opinion of the missionaries Armenian Church authors claim that orthodoxy witnessed by the life of its church to a living faith, and "never impaired nor eclipsed the teachings of Christ."[5] Added to Sarkissian's voice is that of Nerses Apegha whose complaint against the missionaries takes on venomous proportion in the following passage:

> Missionaries . . . should have known well that we had received the sacred responsibility of *evangelism* from the apostles centuries and centuries ago—from the first illuminator. The missionary gentlemen should have known that, during the periods when their forefathers were still living nomadic lives, our forefathers had been able, with the first opportunity even, to understand deeply the meaning of Christ's godly doctrines and had been able to appropriate them. If we were unable to carry on with broad love the work of preaching we had undertaken, its reason must be sought in those political ups-and downs which gave us no opportunity to breathe. Had the missionaries had the heart, the spirit, the calling, they should have leafed through, without fear and dread, the bloody pages of our political history and seen at the top of cathedrals being reconstructed out of blood and fire, the cross of Christ. More! They should have seen in those pages the tortured Armenian priest, the scapegoat of all barbarities, who, after each destruction boldly pulled the rope of the church bell in the name of Christ, for the salvation of souls.[6]

Anyone tampering with this Church and its tradition was one who "led the Armenians astray,"[7] according to Berberian.

In reality, the missionaries had observed in the history of the Armenian nation the validity of this phenomenon. Therefore, it was not that they had failed to learn the history of the nation and the church but they had failed to *appreciate* the symphonic relationship and its benefits. Having come to

4. Garabed Adanalian, *Hooshartzan* (Fresno: Crown Printing Co., 1952), p. 6.

5. Karekin Sarkissian, *The Council of Chalcedon and the Armenian Church*, (London: S.P.C.K., 1965), Prologue.

6. Nerses Apegha Paghdikian, *The Entry of Protestantism into the World of the Dzopk*, (Periodical Agoss, Beirut, Lebanon, Year 12, No. 11 (100), p. 61.

7. Avedis Berberian, *History of Armenians: Beginning with 1772 to 1860.* (Constantinople: Boghos Kirishjian and Co. Press, 1871), p. 295.

the Levant with a Christian mission over which they were excited, they believed that obstacles to the execution of their mission of evangelization were Satan's efforts to block that "God-directed" work. They failed to see that the religio-cultural tradition of the Armenian nation as a whole, and the Armenian Church with its liturgical-sacramental mysteries, had cemented the church and people in such a way so as to create a feeling of partnership—a "community-peopleness" that worked together as one body—and whose disruption would be resented.

The religious, as well as the top lay leadership, therefore, interpreted the work of the American missionaries as a threat to this integrated church-nation unity and so attempted to extirpate the evangelical movement. Some historians find it difficult to blame the Armenian Church altogether for this effort and among them is J. Richter who writes as follows:

> The American mission was more of a threat than perhaps its missionaries realized to the unity of an ancient Church, with whose ecclesiastical organization and with whose historic forms the democratic spirit of American congregationalism was, at best, but little in accord. And with this church unity, which the American Mission thus threatened, was wrapped up the national ideal.[8]

Two of the most prominent of the early missionaries, Goodell and Dwight, appear to be insensitive to the evil of schism.[9] The former speaks about the time "when there will be a tremendous breaking up of those churches, and when they will have to be entirely remodelled"[10] and appears to be happy over "desertions" from the Armenian Church "to the standard of truth."[11] By 1845 Goodell appears to be reconciled to the idea of separation seeing it as a necessity in time, but wants to be sure that the

8. J. Richter, *A History of Protestant Missions in the Near East*, (New York: Fleming H. Revell Co., 1910), p. 112.

9. This insensitivity in all probability is due to their conviction of the validity of their Protestant form of worship not realizing that the worship service of the Armenian Church is heavily Bible-oriented. This writer recently spoke to the highest ecclesiastical authority in the United States, His Grace Archbishop Torkom Manoogian who represents the See of Etchmiadzin in Armenia. He asked him if it were not true that Armenian Protestants, with their emphasis on the Holy Scriptures, had been of some good influence upon the Armenian Church. His comment was that much more of the Scriptures were read in the services of the Armenian Church than in the Protestant. In this connection C.S. Calian in his *Icon and Pulpit* (Philadelphia: The Westminster Press, 1968), page 123 refers to a research study in the Byzantine liturgies of St. John Chrysostom, St. Bazil, and the Presanctified as well as the sacramental services of Baptism, Chrismaton, Holy Unction, and Matrimony in which, he claims, it was discovered that approximately 25 percent of these services consisted of almost direct Biblical material and that the content of the liturgy that alludes to Scripture was even greater. This is also the experience of the writer of this dissertation. The Armenian worship services are heavily Scriptural. The Word is left to speak, not the voice of the preacher interpreting it.

10. Prime, *op. cit.*, p. 174.

11. *Ibid.*, p. 180.

38

action, when it comes, is justifiable.[12] After the separation took place, Goodell felt no pangs of conscience but on the contrary was glad. That is the impression this researcher receives from the following words written soon after the event:

> I did not expect to live to see this day, but I have seen it and am glad. 'This is the day which the Lord hath made, and we will rejoice and be glad in it.' When I removed to Constantinople fifteen years ago, I felt assured either that this day would come, or that the Armenian Church as a body would be reformed; and I never had any anxiety as to the result.[13]

Dwight appears to be equally insensitive to the dangers of a schism. He himself reports an attempt for reconciliation by the Armenian Patriarch Matteos Choohajian. Choohajian had suggested that both the missionaries and the "evangelicals" keep still and avoid all agitation.[14] Dwight's position appears to be stiff in the following words which have been recorded in his book:

> As though such antagonistic elements as the truth of God, and the doctrines and practices of the Armenian Church, could be brought in contact without producing commotion; and honest men, whose sincere desire and purpose was to live always in the fear of God, and to 'maintain consciences void of offence both toward God and toward men,' could readily consent to be led and controlled in their religious conduct, by the worldly, the time-serving, and the unprincipled.[15]

This missionary also speaks very approvingly of converts to the "evangelical" point of view who decided to abstain "from all participation in superstition and idolatry." "They attended regularly upon the ministry of the missionaries," he writes, "and sat down at the table of the Lord with us as guests, because they could neither profitably nor conscientiously unite in this service in the Armenian Churches."[16]

Christian "Mission," like advice, is not acceptable if not requested by the recipient. This is because Christian "Mission" is a form of commitment on the part of the missionary, but a form of "imposition" on the one to whom the missionary goes with his specific beliefs, practices, and doctrines. When one adds to that serious problem an attitude which lacks appreciation of the heritage of another people and also lacks sensitivity to the dangers division might bring to the same people, the cup becomes too full for acceptance. What really happened was that the Armenian Church

12. *Ibid.*, p. 306.
13. *Ibid.*, p. 317.
14. Dwight, *op. cit.*, pp. 217 ff., p. 170.
15. *Ibid.*, pp. 170-171.
16. *Ibid.*, p. 214.

saw the "Mission" as an imposition and the attitude of the missionaries as a threat.

B. Negative Criticism of the Armenian Church

Not only did the missionaries fail to show appreciation of the proud Christian heritage of the Armenians but they became strongly critical of the Armenian Church despite their statements that they were not going to interfere in the beliefs, practices, and traditions of the Armenian Church.

The early records of missionaries Eli Smith and H.G.O. Dwight provided a drastic criticism of the Armenian Church—its beliefs, practices, and traditions.

Following the instructions of January 19, 1830, of the Prudential Committee of the American Board, Smith and Dwight left Malta on March 17[17] and Constantinople on May 21,[18] to research the condition of Armenians. Having gone as far as the spiritual center of Armenia, Etchmiadzin, they returned to Constantinople on May 25, 1831, and to Malta on July 2, 1831.[19] Smith consequently wrote his observations in two volumes and published it in 1833, just two years after the founding of the mission station in Constantinople. However, even before the publication of the book, the reports of the two missionaries reached the Prudential Committee and various sections were published in the Missionary Herald. Spread over the pages of the two volumes as well as in numerous issues of the Herald, there are many negative judgments of the church, the clergy, and the doctrines and ceremonies of the Armenian Church. *These weaknesses did exist, of course, and most of them may be supported by reference to more neutral sources. But, in the light of the statements of neutrality and non-interference by the missionaries, the question arises as to the wisdom of their making highly critical judgments of a people, who, through the centuries, have developed sensitivities and whose major pride lay in the preservation of church and nation.* The two researchers began their negative criticisms with the Armenian Patriarch, stating that his choice or deposition is "a fruitful source of intrigues, strifes, and corruption."[20] They termed "fasting and the cross...the most prominent of the superstitions,"[21] and observances of Sabbath lamentably absent of

17. Eli Smith, *Researches*, Vol. I, p. 44.
18. *Ibid.*, p. 71.
19. *Ibid.*, Vol. II, pp. 328-329.
20. *Ibid.*, Vol. I, p. 57.
21. *Ibid.*, p. 155.

sacredness. [22] They pointed out that other mediators are adopted to the entire exclusion of Christ as the only Mediator;[23] that the prominent trait of the whole nation is love of money;[24] that the forms of worship are "a mummery and an abomination" and "preaching is hardly thought of, and the pulpit is excluded;"[25] that image worship exists to a considerable extent;[26] that worship is "heartless forms of solemn mockery."[27] They described "convents" to be the "very centers of the most unprincipled ambition, of the darkest intrigue, and of the bitterest dissention...places of unchastity...and seats of ignorance,"[28] while they claimed the secular clergy were given to "indolence and the pleasures of the table...gormandizers and hard drinkers."[29] The Eucharist they found to be in the papal tradition of the Church, the Armenians believing in the transubstantiation of the bread and wine into the real body and blood of Christ, instead of regarding it as a simple remembrance of the atoning death of our Savior. [30] Because the prayer used during the auricular confession listed many grave sins, they concluded the recitation of such sins was proof of the nation's immoralities.[31] They criticized the church for believing that baptism and communion are sufficient for salvation; [32] that members ignorantly believed that baptism takes away original sin;[33] that they believed the two essential articles of Christian faith to be the trinity and the divinity of Christ—"The idea of *faith* commonly entertained by the Armenians" being a mere "belief in the Father, and the Son, and the Holy Ghost, in the name of whom they cross themselves. Of justifying faith they have no knowledge; and when it is announced to them, they look upon it as almost as strange a doctrine, as did the philosophers of Athens."[34] Finally, having spent just Friday evening to Tuesday [35] morning at Etchmiadzin, and having witnessed the twentieth anniversary festival of the inauguration of the Catholicos they passed a bitter criticism on all that they had observed, saying: "The whole bore no slight resemblance to a theatrical pantomime, and was evidently calculated, not to be united in as a devotional service, but to be gazed at

22. *Ibid.*
23. *Ibid.*, p. 184.
24. *Ibid.*, p. 213.
25. *Ibid.*, p. 227.
26. *Ibid.*, p. 229.
27. *Ibid.*, p. 230.
28. *Ibid.*, Vol. II, pp. 33-38.
29. *Ibid.*, pp. 44-45.
30. *Ibid.*, p. 102.
31. *Ibid.*, p. 107.
32. *Ibid.*, p. 125.
33. *Ibid.*, p. 126
34. *Ibid.*, p. 124.
35. November 19 to November 23, 1830.

and worshipped....It seemed, in a word, more objectionable in every feature than any papal mass I ever witnessed." [36]

Dwight, the partner or co-traveler of Smith in the Researches into Armenia, and who on completion of the journey was stationed in Constantinople to work with Goodell, wrote his own book in 1854. In this work he was very judgmental of the Armenian Church, claiming at the same time that those who became awakened by being fully convinced of the truth of the evangelical doctrine saw the grave errors of their church. Dwight believed that "most of the ancient books of theology, as well as the most ancient liturgies of the Armenian Church, were strongly tainted with error;" [37] that the Armenian Church followed degenerating tendencies until at length it settled down permanently into hierarchism and formalism, excluded Jesus as mediator and substituted the name of Mary or some other saint, introduced "auricular confession; absolution from sin by the priest; penance; transubstantiation; baptismal regeneration; intercession of the saints and angels; worship of the material cross, of relics, and of pictures; and prayers for the dead." [38] He claimed therefore that such a Church in which "the true gospel scheme of salvation is so entirely overlaid and lost by human inventions, needs a thorough reformation." He saw the scheme of salvation in the Armenian Church to be in error because salvation is considered to be "through what the priest can do" for the believer. That is, the believer "is purified by the priest at baptism, absolved by the priest of his sins, sanctified by the reception of the real body and blood of Christ, transubstantiated by . . . the mysterious agency of an ignorant, and it may be, graceless priest, making salvation possible." [39] In truth, Dwight considered the Armenian Church to be so degenerate as to have become an obstacle for the evangelization of Islam. According to Dwight the Mohammedans (and Jews) did not find it attractive and their prejudice placed them "beyond the possibility of being benefited by any Christian effort in their behalf." [40]

Dwight and Smith have, to all intents and purposes, given a fairly objective analysis of the condition of the Armenian Church. In fact they have some support from other sources. Eutudjian agrees with Dwight's analysis and accepts that many of the "papal abuses" had been embraced. [41] Ricaut, though sympathetic to the Armenian Church, points out that the Armenian Church holds to Baptism as necessary to wash away original sin and Transubstantiation is held as the "papists" do, accepting

36. Eli Smith, *op. cit.*, Vol. II, p. 101.
37. Dwight, *op. cit.*, p. 5.
38. *Ibid.*, pp. 6-7.
39. *Ibid.*, pp. 12-13.
40. Dwight, *op. cit.*, pp. 7-8.
41. Eutudjian, *op. cit.*, p. 48.

This is my Body, and This is my Blood "in their literal sense." [42] He also stresses that there is much emphasis on raising money in the church and excommunication is made use frequently "by the abuse of which the priests procure the most considerable part of their gains." [43] Appleyard, another sympathizer, states the Armenians venerate sacred pictures and the cross, have auricular confession, and raise the Host. [44] Even Southgate, who was to defend the action of the Patriarch in excommunicating the "awakened" evangelicals, accepts the entry of corruptions into the Armenian Church when he writes: "But when the practice of some portions of the Armenians became corrupt, (which has been chiefly through the influence of Rome,) the pictures began to be used for worship, those already in the Churches were not turned into this purpose . . . but others were brought in, chiefly pictures of the Virgin." [45]

Of course, the Armenian Church comes with a serious counter-criticism. This posture is well demonstrated by two modern writers to whom reference has already been made a number of times. Yeghiayan considered the missionary emphasis on salvation through the free grace of God as a missionary tool to "cool the believers from their organized mother church and its ancient authority, by promising them salvation by a direct grace-distribution by God." [46] Supporting a far more extreme position, Nerses Paghdikian saw the purpose of the missionaries to be "to overthrow the ancient classic Armenian and to bring in its place the Holy Bible translated into the spoiled vernacular. To remove the Altar, the mystery of mysteries, and to replace it with a plain podium. To demolish the Armenian-envisioned temples of great antiquity consecrated by the holy blood of Armenian martyrs and to exchange them with a naked and plain house which has no appeal to the mystery-loving soul of the oriental people. . . . To erase from the soul and mind of the Armenian forty centuries-old Traditions by calling them superstitions. . ." [47]

Granting that the missionaries used unacceptable procedures, this researcher also feels that Yeghiayan and Nerses Apegha could be somewhat more sympathetic to the spiritual and pious stance of the missionaries as well as their humanitarian concern. The missionaries were burdened with the problem of making the Armenians appreciate their good intentions and to prove that they had come, as Dwight has stated, from "purely benevolent motives to teach them a better way." [48] Their

42. Paul Ricaut, *The Present State of the Greek and Armenian Churches* (London: John Starkey, 1679), pp. 432-434.
43. *Ibid.*, p. 439.
44. Appleyard, *op. cit.*, pp. 47-49.
45. Horatio Southgate, *State of Christianity in Turkey* (New York: Dana & Co., 1856).
46. Yeghiayan, *op. cit.*, Ch. 9, p. 14. (In published work, p. 216).
47. *Agoss*, Year II, Nos. 8-9-10 (75), p. 152.
48. Dwight, *op. cit.*, p. 179; *Missionary Herald*, January, 1839, p. 41.

unwillingness to understand the predicament of the missionaries indicates that the "language" being spoken by the two sides is quite divergent. We believe Calian understands the predicament both of the missionaries and the Armenian Church when he writes that under the minaret, the social concern of Orthodoxy had been dimmed for the sake of her very survival and "this suppression of outward social consciousness has negatively manifested itself in a ghetto mentality within most Orthodox communities. These communities have been preoccupied with their own survival and have had time for nothing else. . ."[49] In the absence of understanding and confidence on the part of the Armenian Church in the American Mission, the alternative was controversy and possible division.

C. Missionary Activities That Appeared Divisive

To the fundamental and dynamic divergencies written about in the previous two sections were added certain activities on the part of the missionaries which crystallized the differences.

One of these activities was the abandoning of the more cautious policy of the mission vis-a-vis the Armenian Church to a bolder one. Earlier, the missionaries had limited their contacts to personal interviews and the administering of schools. Goodell had limited religious work to Bible studies in his home to twice a week. In 1836, the missionaries commenced a Protestant ministry of public worship service and preaching on a regular basis on Fridays and Sundays, [50] the Friday service being especially for women. [51] As a result, the ecclesiastical rulers of the Armenian Church began to gather up their strength to oppose the progress of the reformation, according to Dwight. [52] It will be granted that this was a natural reaction since the missionaries were introducing a competitive spiritual direction. Even earlier, in 1826, missionary Temple had written to the Secretary of the Board that it was the duty of the missionaries to unveil and expose the abominations of the Papacy, [53] and in February, 1827, as we have noted, Bishop Dionysius Garabedian and Bishop Hagopos of

49. Carnegie Samuel Calian, *Icon and Pulpit* (Philadelphia: The Westminster Press, 1968), pp. 104-105.
50. Eutudjian, *op. cit.*, p. 86.
51. Dwight, *op. cit.*, p. 6.
52. *Ibid.*
53. *A.B.C.F.M., Annual Report,* 1826, p. 92.

Bolou were taken as members into the mission church—an act which made it to be understood that "so far as the mission should be successful, existing ecclesiastical relations were to be broken, and the existing churches destroyed."[54] The bolder policy was crystalized more clearly when in 1841 Armenians in Constantinople were accepted to participate in a communion served to members of five Protestant denominations[55] and on March 4, 1845, in the house of missionary Goodell, communion was administered "in the simple way commanded in the New Testament" to the members of the Union of the Pious.[56] This action was possible, as we see, because in 1844, when Secretary Anderson and Dr. Hawes had visited the Middle East, the ensuing discussions had led to the decision of putting increasing emphasis upon "the organizing of groups of converts into churches, and the laying of responsibility upon them."[57]

The second divisive activity was the establishment of the Union of the Pious[58] in 1836 with twelve members in order to find ways and means for the spreading of views on the reformation of their Church. The Armenian "evangelicals" give the impression that it was their own creation, but we think that it was done in full cooperation with the missionaries. Its existence was apparently known fairly widely, but its activities seem to have borne quite a bit of secrecy—a secrecy supported by the missionaries. Hamlin, in reporting two instances of support of the members in trouble, demonstrates, first, the dependence of the Society upon the missionaries, and second, its secret nature.[59] The support and protection of this Union led the Armenian Church to doubt that the intention of the missionaries was not to split the Church, despite Goodell's claims to the contrary. This and several other attempts at strengthening the "evangelical" cause were considered to be meddling in the affairs of the Armenian Church. Yeghiayan classifies the following five activities under "meddling," the last two of which have been mentioned: (1) the broadening of the Pera elementary school of the mission into a High School and placing newly-converted Der Sahakian as teacher there; (2) the opening of a Girls' High School in Smyrna; (3) the opening of an elementary school in Smyrna; (4) the commencement of Sunday public services in the homes of the missionaries in 1835 for Armenians; (5) and, the founding in 1836 of the group known as the Union of the Pious from the growing like-minded

54. Tracey, op. cit., p. 191; Rufus Anderson, History of the Missions of the A.B.C.F.M. to Oriental Churches (Boston: 1872), Vol. I, p. 47.
55. Prime, op. cit., p. 263.
56. Kassouny, Loossashavigh, p. 35; Eutudjian, op. cit., p. 147.
57. Strong, op. cit., p. 100.
58. Known in Armenian as the "Parebashdoutian Miapanoutune," it was variously translated "The Society of the Pious," "The Evangelical Union," or "The Society of the Godly."
59. For these incidents see Cyrus Hamlin, My Life and Times Among the Turks (New York: Carter, 1878), pp. 29-32 and pp. 135-138.

Armenians around them and which group, with the leadership of the missionaries, Yeghiayan claims, were to enter the battle of separation in 1846.[60]

A third controversial activity was the policy of the missionaries to employ Armenian higher clergy who had renounced their celibate vows to translate the Scriptures into Armenian. In view of the vows of celibacy, a celibate clergy contracting matrimony was not only reputed to be acting unlawfully, but his marriage was invalid.[61] The Armenian populace, therefore, responded with a great emotional resistance when Bishop Dionysius Garabedian, one of the clergy used to translate the Scriptures, visited Smyrna where he was taken by the missionaries to work on translations. Stepan Eutudjian, writing about the visit of the Bishop, explains the resistance in these words:

> But the presence of a married bishop acted as a stumbling-block to the Armenians living in Smyrna, and there arose excitement in the said city. . . . And Dionysius, unable to withstand the excitement, returned to Beirut after a short time.[62]

For this reason, Yeghiayan, assigning the division to the missionaries, says of the celibate higher clergy: "The sad reality arising out of all this is that the missionaries became a haven to unruly and rebel elements to make them serve their purposes."[63] The relationship between the missionaries and the "rebel" Armenian higher clergy roused opposition and from the early beginnings drew the lines of combat.[64]

The fourth divisive activity may be put in the form of a question: Did the American missionaries provide financial advantage in order to convert Armenians of the Apostolic faith to the "evangelical" point of view? Nerses Apegha Paghdikian says that the newly "enlightened" Armenians were men of base intentions, who, having joined the missionaries for the money-motive "had turned into perverse plate-lickers"[65] in the name of a piece of bread. Yeghiayan argues that the missionaries hired the two earliest converts, Hovhannes Der Sahakian and Senekerim Der Minassian as teachers in their school at Pera on a specific condition, "that condition

---

60. Yeghiayan, *op. cit.*, Chapter 9, pp. 8-10. (In published work, pp. 210-212).

61. James Issaverdens, *The Sacred Rites and Ceremonies of the Armenian Church* (Venice: St. Lazarre Press, 1876), p. 447.

62. Eutudjian, *op. cit.*, p. 59.

63. Yeghiayan, *op. cit.*, Ch. 8, p. 24. (In published work, p. 196).

64. Goodell accepted his action of the use of the Bishops as a mistake when he wrote in 1835: "When I first came into these countries, I laid hold of individuals, and endeavored to pull them out of the fire; but my aim is now to take hold of whole communities, and, as far as possible, to raise them up to 'sit together in heavenly places in Christ.' "

65. Nerses Paghdikian, *Agoss*, Year 12, No. 6 (83), p. 77.

being adherence to protestantism." [66] Eutudjian, on the other hand, assigns the employment to worth—to the spiritual condition of the two early converts, while Senekerim in his autobiographical narration assigns the conversion to their "developing evangelical views," "committing their lives to Christ," "consecrating themselves to the reformation of the Armenian people." [67] Missionary Goodell claims the young men went to him for help and he endeavored "to do them all the good" in his power. [68]

On the objective side, we can point to three situations which appear to make the missionary vulnerable to the "accusation." The first instance is Goodell's custom in Beirut when he would go out with Bishop Dionysius Garabedian on Wednesdays and Saturdays to give public religious instruction to beggars. He talks about "taking the Bible under one arm, and the basket of bread under the other" and going to a well where he would read a portion of Scripture, the Bishop would address the beggars on the subject of religion, and then they would distribute the bread and send them away in peace. [69]

In addition to the employment of the two earliest converts, it seems that others who became sympathetic to the point of view of the missionaries were similarly employed. Bishop Dionysius and Bishop Hagop were so employed. Others were Mr. Sarkis and Mr. Mugurditch Thomesean. [70]

The third reference is to Cyrus Hamlin who established a workshop for the boys of Bebek Seminary for sheet-iron stoves and stove-pipes. Acknowledging that there was gratuitous aid, he wrote that "Gratuitous aid was becoming a failure and a disease" and developed an economic policy which believed that "Aiding the poor with money directly is so bad a policy, that nothing but necessity can ever justify it." [71] Hamlin, by his objection to the practice, appears to accept its existence.

These are doubtful and divisive approaches, but it may not be fair to "accuse" the missionaries of base motives in their efforts to revitalize the Christian life of individuals. There were genuine cases of belief by conviction some of whom relinquished employment, estate, and offers of great wealth. [72] *The "accusation" that conversion may have a socio-economic basis may be true of some, but may not be an entirely valid answer to "Awakening."* Wach writes of this fact rather pointedly in the following passage:

66. Yeghiayan, *op. cit.*, Ch. 9, pp. 3-4. (In published work, p. 204)
67. *Missionary Herald*, Volume XXXII, January, 1836, pp. 30-32.
68. *Ibid.*, p. 33.
69. *Missionary Herlad*, pp. 272-273; *A.B.C.F.M. Annual Report, 1825, p. 88.*
70. *A.B.C.F.M. Annual Report*, 1845, p. 86.
71. Hamlin, *op. cit.*, pp. 212-213; p. 99.
72. For such cases see, Prime, *op. cit.*, pp. 181, 263-265; Dwight, *op. cit.*, pp. 150, 233; Strong, *op. cit.*, pp. 211, 219.

On the other hand, it has become popular to explain sectarianism as a result of predominantly or even exclusively economic and social factors and conditions. Though there is some truth in this theory, it should not be pressed to the point of ignoring the genuine religious experiences which more often than not supply the initial impulse.[73]

Nevertheless, the Armenians believed that the missionaries were operating on that basis. When they noted some "convert" whose zeal for some reason cooled, they cast the most humiliating personal remark in these Turkish words: "Oun Var, Din Var; Oun Bitdee, Din Bitdee."[74]

As we conclude Part I of this research, we must sum up what really happened to bring on the separation. The religious tradition with which the missionaries came to the Armenians was diametrically opposed to that of the Armenian Church. The purpose, goal and design of the American Mission, idealistic and helpful as they might have seemed for the missionaries, was interpreted as an imposition by the Armenian Church. Finally, the attitude and activities of the missionaries on the field were seen as unsympathetic and divisive. All of which has led this writer to find it difficult to accept the statement of Secretary Barton that "The missionaries made no attacks upon churches, their customs, or beliefs, but strove by positive, quiet effort to show the leaders how much they lacked and to help them bring about the necessary changes . . . . When the separation did come, it was in spite of every effort of the missionaries to prevent it."[75] The events and policies enumerated do not sustain this position.

It is our opinion that the missionaries would have done better to state that it was in the nature of missionary work that adherents would have to be won: that it was in the nature of the theology of missions that once the Gospel was disseminated, grave controversial subjects would have to be grappled with. The missionaries knew this in the depth of their hearts. Their weakness and frailty made them fearful to say that more emphatically and clearly, yet in love. The clearer statement of their purposes to the Armenian Church might not have avoided the separation that came, but it would have helped them not to think one thing and do another—as the records lead us to think they did. The good they did would have been the same. In fact, a fair evaluation of the total work of the missionaries demonstrates that their contribution to the spiritual, intellectual, and social life of Armenians in the Ottoman Empire is incalculable.[76]

73. Wach, *op. cit.*, p. 203.

74. "There is flour, there is faith; flour is no more, faith is no more." This expression means that so long as there is material gain, there was an acknowledgement of faith. As soon as material assistance was stopped, the recipient returned to his former condition.

75. *Supra*, Chapter I, pp. 1-2.

76. For a masterful defense of the great positive contributions of Americans to Armenian life see Yervant Y. Hadidian's "The American Influence in The Background of Armenians." (Preserved in the archives of the Armenian Missionary Association of America, Inc.).

PART TWO

THE RESPONSE OF THE
ARMENIAN APOSTOLIC CHURCH

CHAPTER V

A SHORT HISTORY OF REFORM TRENDS IN THE ARMENIAN CHURCH

A. *Conversion of Armenia and the Early Armenian Church*

By the edict of King Tiridates in 301 A.D. Christianity became the state religion of pagan Armenia, "anticipating Constantine's Edict of Toleration (313) by a dozen years,"[1] and Gregory the Illuminator, the founder of the Armenian Church, was ordained as Archbishop and Catholicos of Armenia in 302 A.D. On his ordination Gregory himself consecrated "four hundred bishops, and an immense number of priests."[2] When, in addition to the abundant availability of clergy thus ordained, is added the historical evidence that under at least three kings of Armenia Christians were persecuted unto death in 110, 230, and 287[3] it becomes reasonable to believe that prior to the acceptance of Christianity as a state religion there must have been an existing Christianity in Armenia.

As a matter of fact, the Armenian Church Fathers were convinced that the first preachers of the Christian Gospel in Armenia were St. Thaddeus and St. Bartholemew and that the legends of the correspondence of King Abgarus of Edessa with Christ[4] and the martyrdom of the virgins Kayyane and Hripsime were true.[5] This traditional claim for the apostolic origins of Armenian Christianity, however, has been challenged on historical grounds because the early documents are hagiographical pieces of

---

1. Leon Arpee, *A History of Armenian Christianity* (Princeton: Princeton University Press, 1946), p. 15.
2. M. Chamchean, *History of Armenia*. J. Avdall's translation. (Calcutta: Bishop's College Press, 1827), Vol. I, p. 162.
3. Arpee, *op. cit.*, p. 9.
4. Eusibius, *The Church History*, in *A Select Library of the Nicene and Post-Nicene Fathers of the Christian Church* (ed. P. Schaff and H. Wace (2nd series); New York: The Christian Literature Co., 1890), I, 100 ff., 291; F.C. Burkitt, *Early Eastern Christianity* (London: John Murray, 1904), pp. 11-20.
5. Tertullian, *Latin Christianity: Its Founder, Tertullian, in the Ante-Nicene Fathers. Translations of the Fathers down to* A.D. 325 (ed. A. Roberts and J. Donaldson. American reprint of the Edinburgh Edition; revised; Buffalo: The Christian Literature Publishing Co., 1885), III, 157 ff.; Ormanian, *National History*, Vol. I, Columns 1-70; Arpee, *op. cit.*, pp. 9 ff.

literature and cannot be relied upon as historical documents.[6] It has been suggested instead that the conversion of Armenia was rather the result of a gradual process having its roots in the rapid advance of Christianity in the second and third centuries.[7]

Regarding the character of early Armenian Christianity, there is a divergence of opinion. Armenian Orthodox writers of the fifth century studiously ignore the earlier Christianity of their land. They paint the picture of Armenian Christianity begun by Gregory the Illuminator. Conybeare, on the other hand, has argued that early Armenian Christianity was Ebionitic or Judaistic in character[8] which Leon Arpee finds plausible.[9] In the Appendix to *The Key of Truth* Conybeare provides in English translation the "Letter of Macarius," Bishop of Jerusalem, written sometime between 325 and 335 in which the following picture emerges about the character of the Christianity of the period: (1) that there was opposition to the use of fonts and even deacons administered the baptismal rite; (2) that diocesan bishops were unpopular and the clergy were on an equal footing; (3) that communion was observed more as a Jewish paschal rite, with the "mixed" cup, than as a Christian sacrament with the "unmixed wine."[10] These trends appear to be pointing to the direction of Adoptionism as held by the later Paulicians,[11] one important internal evidence being the practice of the Armenian Church which holds the feasts of Nativity and Baptism on the same day—January 6, the day of Epiphany.

Adanalian argues for the existence of "pure" and "simple" Apostolic preaching and teaching before Christianity by royal edict was made the state religion. He states that this "pure" and "simple" Apostolic tradition was suppressed by Gregory the Illuminator, the founder of the Armenian Apostolic Church, who had received his clerical training in the Greek Orthodox tradition in Cappadocia.[12]

At least one evidence is not questionable, and that is regarding the practice of celibacy. Up to the end of the fifth century, the Catholici of the Armenian Church were married men, indicating that the Armenian Church came to introduce changes in its discipline and theology over its

---

6. K. Sarkissian, *The Council of Chalcedon and the Armenian Church* (London: S.P.C.K., 1965), pp. 76-78.

7. *Ibid.*, p. 79; Arpee, *op. cit.*, p. 9.

8. F.C. Conybeare, *The Key of Truth: A Manual of the Paulician Church of Armenia* (Oxford: Clarendon Press, 1898), pp. xc ff.

9. Leon Arpee, *op. cit.*, p. 9. (For a short review of the character of the early Christianity in Armenia see pp. 9-15).

10. F.C. Conybeare, Appendix, "Letter of Macarius."

11. Arpee, *op. cit.*, p. 14.

12. Garabed Adanalian, Unpublished work, preserved in manuscript before his death and now in the hands of his daughter in Washington, D.C.

earlier practices. Aristakes and Vertanes, sons of Gregory, followed him to the hierarchal episcopacy established by their father. Vertanes' son, Housik, became the next successor after whom the office passed on to a disciple, Paren (348-352). After Paren, the office went back to Gregory's family—to his grandson Nerses the great (353-373),[13] under whose son Sahag (387-436) the Armenian alphabet was formulated by St. Mesrop to provide the Scriptures to the general public, and the Bible was translated in 411. This event helped lay the foundation of a Golden Age in literature in the same century,[14] which also gave the total Armenian population a deeper understanding of the Scriptures and of Christianity. (Armenian church authorities claim, however, that all married clergy who became Catholici had lost their wives previously).

The vitality of the early Church is also seen in the mission-mindedness of the Armenian Church. Chakmakjian documents this mission-mindedness by showing that Gregory the Illuminator, his son Gregoris, and several of his successors preached the Gospel to the Georgians, Albanians, Persians, Assyrians, Jews, Huns and pagans.[15] Kassouny, too, demonstrates the mission-mindedness of the early Armenian Church leaders in his *Missionary Spirit in the Armenian Church*[16] and like Chakmakjian argues that this spirit was weakened finally due to the nationalization of the Armenian Church as well as its ceremonialism, sacerdotalism, and doctrinal controversies.[17]

B. Isolationism and Nationalization of the Armenian Church

The outreach of the Armenian Church weakened gradually due to grave historical events. One of these was the Council of Chalcedon, which the Armenian Church leaders were unable to attend since the nation was at war in 451 with Persia. Later on, the church was unable to accept the formula of the Council on the nature of Christ and after fifty-five or fifty-

13. Arpee, *op. cit.*, pp. 9-23; Ormanian, *National History* (Jerusalem: St. James Press, 1927), Cols. 71-222.
14. Ormanian, *op. cit.*, Cols. 123-222; Arpee, *op. cit.*, pp. 24-42; Chamchean, *History of Armenia* (Calcutta: Calcutta Bishop's Press, 1827), pp. 233-240; A.A. Bedikian, *Golden Age of Armenian Literature* (Armenian Missionary Association of America, Inc., 1964).
15. Hagop A. Chakmakjian, *Armenian Christology and Evangelization of Islam*, (Leiden: E.J. Brill, 1965), pp. 59-62.
16. Translated by the Armenian Missionary Association of America, Inc. under the title *Trail Blazers at Dawn.*
17. Yeghia S. Kassouny, *Missionary Spirit in the Armenian Church* (Aleppo: Bozolokian Press, 1940), pp. 1-23; *Trail Blazers at Dawn* (Translation of the Armenian Missionary Association of America, Inc. (New York: undated), pp. 1-18.

seven years, depending on whether the Synod of Dowin was held in 506 or 508 A.D., the Armenian Church broke with the main stream of Christianity. [18] According to Sarkissian, the event was of crucial importance in the history of the Armenian Church because it determined not only its doctrinal position within the entire Christian world but also affected immensely the political life of the Armenian people, the character and orientation of theological literature, and the temper of the religious leadership. The decision led to "doctrinal disputations, ecclesiastical quarrels, and political entanglements of the most difficult and complicated nature." [19] The disastrous consequences were, according to Sarkissian, that they led to isolation resulting "in hard, staunch, exclusive, unyielding attitudes." [20] What the Synod had determined amounted to the following important trends: that the Armenian Church is "anti-dyophysite in its basic principle and anti-Nestorian in its outward expression;" that it accepts the "sufficiency of the Council of Nicea" and "the three Ecumenical Councils;" that it rejects with unyielding opposition the "Antiochian or Nestorian theologians;" and, above all, it appropriates "Cyril's christological teaching as embodied in the twelve Anathematisms, accompanied by an adherence to Zeno's Henoticon." [21]

Hagop A. Chakmakjian, also, having the anti-Chalcedon position of the Armenian Church in mind, argues in his doctrinal dissertation published in 1965 that the Monophysite position of the Apostolic Church brought disastrous consequences. He believes that the Monophysite Christology of the Church caused the break of the Armenian Church with the Church of the Empire, turning it schismatic and forcing it to become self-defensive, isolationist, dogmatic, ceremonialistic, sacramentarian and sacerdotarian; that the defensive isolationism led it to neglect the opportunity for aggressive evangelism in their non-Christian environment; that the complete break with the Church of the Empire, the consequent persecutions, and the need for self-defense fully nationalized the Church; and, ultimately, the religious isolationism and nationalism led to political isolationism.[22] Chakmakjian's burden is to demonstrate that the monophysite position led to some consequences which ultimately *created* and *preserved* the Church of Armenia but led it to trespass the boundaries of Christian vocation and to enter the realm of aggressive nationalism and politics. So he sums up his argument in these words:

---

18. Karekin Sarkissian, *The Council of Chalcedon and the Armenian Church* (London: S.P.C.K., 1965), pp. 196-218.
19. Sarkissian, *op. cit.*, pp. 196-218.
20. *Ibid.*
21. *Ibid.*, pp. 210-212.
22. Hagop A. Chakmakjian, *Armenian Christology and the Evangelization of Islam* (Leiden: E.J. Brill, 1965), pp. 7-8.

The Armenian Church, first alienated from the church in Caesarea on administrative and jurisdictional as well as national considerations, finally broke with the Church of the Empire on Christological grounds. Christology became instrumental in segregating the Armenian Christians and in preserving their Church as a national heritage. The Armenian Church, self-isolated by Christological position and nationalized to withstand Greek persecutions, encroachments, and assimilation, endeavored to preserve the nation intact. This it accomplished by conserving the Armenian language, literature, and traditions amidst alien peoples, cultures, and religions. The doctrinally isolated and ecclesiastically nationalized church identified itself with the aspirations of the Armenian nation and ventured into the field of aggressive politics. . . . Consequently . . . the divine verdict was pronounced. . . . By insisting on its Monophysite Christology, the Armenian Church had isolated itself from the world church. By self-isolation, it had become a national, self-contained, and defensive church. By identifying itself with the national aspirations of the race, it had ventured into the field of politics where it had encountered the ultranationalism of Turkish Pan-Turanianism. And in religion, by Christ-worship it confronted the fanaticism of the ultra-monotheistic Ulamas and Mullas.[23]

To read the history of Chamchean from the seventh century and on, a history from "the creation of the world according to the Septuagint, 2663 B.C." to 1780 A.D.,[24] with an appended portion up to 1827, is to take pity upon the nation. Persian humiliations and pressures, Seljuk plunderings and murders, Saracen maraudings, Turkish atrocities following one upon another simply crushed the nation. Despite all, the nation stayed true to the faith of Christ.[25]

23. Hagop A. Chakmakjian, *op. cit.*, pp. 105, 107.
Chakmakjian has presented a convincing argument, but it is problematic to agree with him that the evangelization of Islam failed due to the monophysite Christology of the Church. The problem arises out of the fact that the Nestorians, living in similar regions as the Armenians, also failed to win the Moslems over to Christianity. We concur with him, however, that the Armenian Church turned strongly nationalistic and as a result developed staunch, exclusive, and unyielding attitudes. The missionaries had to contend with this theological, cultural, and national unyielding attitude. From the outset, therefore, historical evidences arose to make the separation inevitable.
24. The early portions of Chamchean's history are weakened by a dependence upon legend, and his title which assigns creation to 2663 B.C. raises questions about his right to be a historian. However, outside these two weaknesses, his historical reflections upon the life of the Armenian nation have obtained the reasonable attention of Armenian historians.
25. Chamchean, *op. cit.*, pp. 373 in Vol. I to the end of Vol. II.
This kind of faithfulness led missionary critique of the Armenian Church, Eli Smith, who presented a dark picture of the Armenian Church, to write: "and should any of the pictures of semi-barbarism and demoralization, which will occasionally be given, tend to excite disgust, such a feeling will be turned into the most charitable compassion, by a view of the wars, persecutions, lawless cruelty, and systematic oppression which have rolled over, or rested upon Armenia, and crushed its inhabitants to the dust. Indeed, if the reader's reflections take the same course as the author's, he will wonder, not so much that the Armenians have merely the name of Christianity, as that they have even that. . . . The best fruit of religion that is presented to us, is the unyielding steadfastness with which Magian and Mohammedan persecutions were endured, to the loss of property, of liberty, and often of life." (Smith, *Researches*, pp. 13, 32)

C. Resistance Against the Established Church

The first organized and strong resistance against the established Armenian Church came from the Paulician-Tonrakian movement which showed adoptionist-unitarian strain of the so-called Monarchian type that some have suggested was evident among Armenians in the first three centuries. [26] The movement extended in time from the middle of the seventh to the middle of the ninth century for the Paulician portion, and from the middle of the ninth to the middle of the eleventh for the Tonrakian portion. [27] It was almost after complete annihilation that the sect showed itself active again under Smbat in the village of Tonrak, from where they received the last-stated name. Joining the great exodus at the end of the Russo-Turkish War of 1828-1829, many Tonrakians settled in Russian-Armenia. In the period between 1837-1845 the Synod of Etchmiadzin held an inquest into the tenets and usages of the sect at which time a manuscript volume was seized from the sectaries, *The Key of Truth*. This Armenian text turned out to be "a copy of a copy" made in 1782 from a lost sample by a certain John Vartabedian. Conybeare published the text in 1898 with an Introduction and Translation. The *Key*, suggesting their roots might be in Paul of Samosota, makes it clear that the Paulicians and the subsequent Tonrakians were Unitarian Anabaptists believing Christ to have become the Head of a New Creation by worth and by obtaining adult baptism. [28]

Arpee and Conybeare both demonstrate that the beliefs of the Paulician sect [29] were diametrically opposed to the traditions and beliefs of the Armenian Church. Against the belief of the Church that Mary was a

26. Frederick C. Conybeare, *The Key of Truth: Manual of the Paulician Church of Armenia* (Oxford: Clarendon Press, 1898), pp. xc ff.; Kevork-Mesrob, *The Entry of Christianity Among the Armenians Before Gregory the Illuminator*, (Constantinople: O. Arzooman, 1910), pp. 7-23.

27. For the origin of this obscure sect, the persecution of its leaders, and their influence see the following: F.L. Cross, *The Oxford Dictionary of the Christian Church*, "Paulicians." (London: Oxford University Press, 1958), p. 1035; Leon Arpee, *The Armenian Awakening* (Chicago: The University of Chicago Press, 1909), pp. 63-92; F.C. Conybeare, *The Key of Truth*, (Oxford: Clarendon Press, 1898), Introduction; K. Ter-Mkrttschian, *Die Paulikianer im byzantinischen Kaiserreich und verwandte ketzerische Erscheinungen in Armenia* (1893, with Armenian sources); and for their influence on the Bogomiles, see D. Obolensky, *The Bogomiles. A Study in Balkan Manichaeism* (1948). For a treatment of the Paulician movement from a Marxian point of view, wherein the movement is seen as the revolt of the peasantry against the status-quo, see Melik-Pakhishian, *The Paulician Movement in Armenia* (Yerevan: University of Yerevan, 1953). For a recent treatment (in Armenian language) see Arsen A. Goergizian's work on the Paulicians.

28. Arpee, *op. cit.*, pp. 101-118; Conybeare, *op. cit.*, pp. 67-124.

29. Arpee, however, takes pains to point out that Manichaeism and Paulicianism must not be confused despite the fact that there are a few points of contact between the two. See Arpee's *A History of Armenian Christianity*, pp. 102-105.

perpetual virgin, the sectarians maintained that she bore other children after Jesus. The Paulicians also rejected the intercession of the saints, condemned the veneration of the cross, and denounced the hierarchy of the Church as unscriptural. Further, they censured the worship and ordinances of the Church, accepting only the spiritual intent of baptism and the Lord's Supper. [30] For such beliefs and others, they endured "scourgings, imprisonments, tortures, reproaches, sufferings, and all the tribulations of the world." [31]

The Paulician-Tonrakian movement was crushed in its effectiveness. The combined strength of state and church was able to perform that task between the seventh and the eleventh centuries.

However, resistance to the "errors" of the Armenian Church showed itself again in the eighteenth century with the criticism of priest Dibajian. A prominent Armenian historian wrote the following about him:

> But long before the coming of the Protestant missionaries to the East, an Armenian priest in 1760 had raised a voice regarding the reformation of the Armenian Church. [32]

Priest Dibajian is given the honor of being the first in modern times to attempt the reformation of the Armenian Church. In an unpublished book, he had exposed the glaring errors of his Church, the inconsistencies in faith, practice and conduct of the priests and bishops, and the superstition of the people. He had tested every principle and ceremony against the high standard of the Bible, with the exception of the doctrine of justification by faith to which he had made no allusion. Of this unpublished book copies ". . . were secretly kept by individuals; and, at the beginning of the present reformation in the Armenian Church, they were providentially brought to light, and used to much advantage in directing the attention of people to the prevailing errors of the Church." [33] Priest Dibajian raised his voice while at the Samatia quarter of Constantinople and hand-written copies of his book found circulation until 1820. [34] According to Kassouny, Dibajian's reflections about the past showed evidences that the fourth and early mid-fifth century Armenian Church had a simple, Apostolic form of worship, and was considered to be "a fellowship of believers" [35] and not a hierarchy of priests. After the fifth century elements not in agreement with that spirit had made entry into the

---

30. *Ibid.*, pp. 101-118.
31. Conybeare, *op. cit.*, (Armenian Text), p. 44.
32. Kevork-Mesrob. Article in *Hairenik Amsakeer* (monthly), 1934, No. 11, p. 95.
33. Dwight, *op. cit.*, p. 17.
34. Kassouny, *Loossashavigh*, p. 4.
35. *Ibid.*

Church. [36] The early nineteenth-century condition of the Armenian Church, therefore, was at a low spiritual ebb. According to Arpee, the Church was totally ceremonial, for he says:

> Superstition, ceremonialism, and priest-craft prevailed. The veneration of anointed crosses, of pictures and relics of saints, the giving of alms, the observance of penance, fasts, and vigils, and the going on pilgrimages to Etschmiadzin and Jerusalem, to most Armenians constituted the sum and substance of religion. Preaching in the Armenian church was very un-common. The parish priest never preached. Most of the preaching was done by vartabeds, sent out from Etschmiadzin, Jerusalem, and other monastic centers, with whom it was partly a matter of reciting the virtues of relics and recounting of legends of saints, and largely a matter of appealing for contributions. The Bible was not generally read. [37]

There were calls for reforms, therefore, which the American missionaries noted carefully and which author Strong summed up thus:

> The missionaries discovered that there were already signs of awakening in the Gregorian Church; reformers and religious enthusiasts had striven to break through its formalism. [38]

What has to be noted is that there has always been a desire for refor-mation in the Armenian ethos, and that chiefly due to dissatisfaction with the traditions and practices of the Armenian Church. Yeghiayan himself, writing to negate the influence of the missionaries, accepts that for cen-turies the matter of the reformation of the Church was a living issue and that in the nineteenth century the Armenians had entered into the path of unusual 're-blossoming.' [39]

D. Need for Revitalization

In early nineteenth century there was need for revitalization—a need which had been stimulated as a result of a "renaissance" [40] of knowledge, language, and religion. [41] In a doctoral dissertation which was published in 1964, James Etmekjian claims that it was with the founding by Mkhitar

---

36. *Ibid.*
37. Arpee, *Awakening*, p. 12.
38. William Ellsworth Strong, *The Story of the American Board: An Account of the First Hundred Years* (Boston: The Pilgrim Press, 1910), p. 91.
39. Yeghiayan, *op. cit.*, Introduction. p. 4.
40. A revival of older and ancient literature.
41. H.M. Janashian, *History of Contemporary Armenian Literature* (Venice: St. Lazarre, 1953), pp. 1-13.

Sepasdatsi of his new Armenian Catholic order in 1701 in Pera, Constantinople, that "renaissance" in linguistic, religious, educational and historical literature took a leap forward. Father Mkhitar, both a zealous religious leader and a zealous patriot produced a grammar of the Armenian vernacular and a monumental *Dictionary of the Armenian Language*. His followers carried on his religious and linguistic work and expanded their activity to the fields of history, geography, and archaeology. The Mkhitarists also revived the Armenian Classics so that by 1836, inaccessible manuscripts were in readable volumes. Added to these developments was the revival of the press beginning in 1794 in India and spreading to Constantinople. Finally, there was the "exodus" to France of young men for the purpose of study. By 1839 a veritable stream of students had moved from Constantinople to France and back to Constantinople. Lycees, institutes, and universities in Paris opened their doors to future Armenian doctors, architects, engineers, teachers, government workers, businessmen, journalists, translators, and secretaries. The eighteenth and the first half of the nineteenth centuries brought about a gradual awakening of the Armenian people, the intellectuals having a consuming desire to help their people to wake up and to recapture the glory of their past. Some of these men, such as Hovhannes Deroyentz (1801-1888) interpreted patriotism to mean a fanatical defense of the Armenian Church. The latter, for instance, the best informed man on religious matters, became the champion of the conservatives and defended old religious traditions vehemently.[42]

Constantinople, therefore, a great Metropolis which contained a great variety of peoples as well as a ferment of intellectual movement, became a point where Armenian reform tendencies converged. There were from 100,000 to 200,000 Armenians in Constantinople in 1800. Intellectual awakening induced questioning in all areas of life; economic well-being brought on more independent thinking. Exposition to Europeans and European ways stimulated desire for better ways of life. This revival of thinking on all fronts suggested a parallel revival in the religious area. As A. Shmavonian remarks, "The religious life of the nation had as much need for progress, in terms of freedom, as the intellectual, economic, or social."[43]

In respect for the need for revitalization reference needs to be made to Anthony F.C. Wallace's statement of what he calls "Revitalization Movement."[44] Wallace proposes the term "Revitilization" for the

---

42. James Etmekjian, *The French Influence on the Western Armenian Renaissance.* (New York: Twayne Publishers, Inc., 1964), pp. 53-137.
43. S. Eutudjian, *op. cit.*, Introduction, p. d.
44. Anthony F.C. Wallace, "Revitalization Movements," *American Anthropologist,* LVIII (1956), pp. 264-279.

uniform process of major cultural-system innovations such as "nativistic movement," "reform movement," "religious revival," "sect formation," "social movement," "revolution," and defines it "as a deliberate, organized, conscious effort by members of a society to construct a more satisfying culture." [45] He believes that it is "functionally necessary for every person in society to maintain a mental image of the society and its culture, as well as of his own body and its behavioral regularities, in order to act in ways which reduce stress at all levels of the system." [46] Thus, whenever an individual "under chronic, physiologically measurable stress receives information that his mental image does not lead to action which reduces the level of stress, he must choose between maintaining his present mazeway (mental image) and tolerating the stress, or changing the mazeway in an attempt to reduce the stress." [47] This is one condition under which the revitalization movement occurs. The other condition under which it occurs is a disillusionment with a distorted cultural *Gestalt*, so that changing one's mental image involves changing the total *Gestalt* of his image of self, society, and culture, of nature and body, and of ways of action. Further, "The movement is usually conceived in a prophet's revelatory visions, which provide for him a satisfactory relationship to the supernatural and outline a new way of life under divine sanction." [48]

There is an important relationship of this interpretation to our study. The Armenian in Turkey had a rather disturbed mental image of the society in which he lived. Trampled underfoot for centuries, persecuted, and considered to be a third class citizen in his own native land occupied by a tyrannical government, he was under great stress. With the stirrings of changes under reforming Sultans giving him the right to 'liberty of life' and with the hope for a renewed life witnessed to him by the newly-arrived missionaries, the Armenian was ready to burst out of his confining shell. Failure to understand this need for image change and *Gestalt* satisfaction by his own religio-civic community, the head of which was his own Armenian patriarch, stiffened positions to such an extent as to add another cause leading to separation. As Wallace observes, "Most denominational and sectarian groups and orders budded or split off after failure to revitalize a traditional institution." [49]

We would not be far from the truth if we stated that failure to revitalize the traditional Armenian Church and institution became a basic factor

45. *Ibid.*, p. 279.
46. *Ibid.*, p. 266.
47. *Ibid.*, p. 267.
48. *Ibid.*, p. 279.
49. *Ibid.*, p. 267.

leading to separation, for one cannot block the religious dreams of men, even if those dreams might be judged to be anti-nationalistic or anti-patriotic. Of this truth, neither the Armenian community in general, nor the religious leadership in particular was conscious. But the braver souls, or, in the judgment of the anti-reformation leaders, the mean pecuniary souls, deeply felt and wanted its realization. To block this need was to ask for trouble.

CHAPTER VI

GROWING RESISTANCE AGAINST THE MISSIONARIES

The Armenian Church has throughout its history held a firm attitude towards doubtful doctrinal positions. It held true to that historic posture in the case of the American Board and its missionaries.

A. The Reign of Five Patriarchs

Five Armenian Patriarchs reigned during the period of our discussion, namely from about 1830 to 1846. Patriarch Garabed of Istanbul resigned on September 4, 1831[1] and was succeeded by Patriarch Stepanos, named the 'Dove' for his kindly temperament. He was broad-minded and permissive, characteristics which enabled him to be sympathetic towards the work of the American missionaries. Hagopos replaced him by intrigue on March 13, 1839,[2] having first, on February 5, 1839, been made "Pokhanort"[3] to the incumbent.[4] It was during his patriarchate that the first round of persecution began. But Hagopos soon fell from the patriarchate, opening the way for the return of Stepanos. Bishop Boghos, prelate of Smyrna became Stepanos' "Pokhanort." This event took place on September 15, 1840.[5] But a year later, namely on September 19, 1841, Stepanos resigned again and went to his former diocese of the monastery of Armash. In his place was elected Constantinople-born Bishop Asdvadzadoor.[6] Following the national conference of July 1, 1844, Patriarch Asdvadzadoor resigned and archbishop Matteos Choohajian, prelate of Smyrna, was elected and was confirmed by the usual governmental decree.[7] Before his resignation, he had become openly intolerant of the

---

1. Avedis Berberian, *History of Armenians: Beginning with 1772 to 1860* (Constantinople: Boghos Kirishjian & Co. Press, 1871), p. 484.
2. *Ibid.*, p. 497.
3. May be translated "assistant," "deputy," "substitute," "representative," or "one in line to replace."
4. Berberian, *op. cit.*, p. 497.
5. *Ibid.*, p. 502; Dwight, *op. cit.*, p. 109.
6. Berberian, *op. cit.*, pp. 502 f.
7. *Ibid.*, p. 521. (According to an early agreement, all appointed Patriarchs had to be confirmed by the Sultan).

Evangelicals and said that he would give himself no rest until the "offensive heresy" was rooted out. "May the curse of God be upon them; may they all be destroyed," he invoked with vengeance.[8] Matteos Choohajian, as early as 1832, had been on friendly terms with the missionaries while he was a 'Vartabed" around the Bosphorus region. Visits had been exchanged and he had informed William G. Schauffler that there were a number of "inquiring, doubting, and seeking" Jews but that they were persecuted.[9] Goodell and Dwight owed their early information about Armenian customs, history, and religion to "Vartabed" Matteos.[10] His teacher, the famed Peshtimaljian, described Matteos as "a man of enlightened views, but without principle, and always governed by what he considered the prevailing opinions and wishes of those whom he desired to please. When thrown among men of the ritual party, he was a ritualist, and when among evangelical men, he became evangelical."[11] It was during his Patriarchate that the separation would take place in 1846. On October 1, 1848, wearied of the ingratitude of several *Amiras* who were defaming him with unjust slander, he turned in his resignation[12] and was replaced by Patriarch Hagopos.

B. Changing Relationships

Generally speaking, the Armenian higher clergy accepted the American missionaries respectfully.[13] There is the instance when on January 14, 1832, the missionaries visited Patriarch Stepan for the first time.[14] They were received cordially and with great honor.[15] During this visit the Patriarch agreed to provide some schoolmasters or priests to learn the Lancastrian system of education for the purpose of opening schools[16] and assigned Paul Physica (Paul the Philosopher) for this purpose.[17] Early

8. Dwight, *op. cit.*, pp. 166-167.
9. Choules, *op. cit.*, p. 311.
10. Eutudjian, *op. cit.*, p. 47.
11. Dwight, *op. cit.*, pp. 169-170.
12. Berberian, *op. cit.*, pp. 560-561.
13. But it is not clear that they were accepted without fear or doubt. Both sides claim, for different reasons, that cordial relationships existed at first. The missionaries say they were received cordially in order to demonstrate that the Armenian higher clergy changed their mind mysteriously. The Armenian Church sources say the missionaries were received respectfully in order to demonstrate that the missionaries violated the trust that was put on them.
14. Eutudjian erroneously assigns this visit to be during the Patriarchate of Garabed.
15. Eutudjian, *op.cit.*, p. 49; Prime, *op. cit.*, p. 132; Dwight, *op. cit.*, p. 32; Kherlopian, *op. cit.*, p. 6; *A.B.C.F.M. Annual Report*, 1832, p. 66.
Dwight, *op. cit.*, p. 32; Eutudjian, *op. cit.*, p. 50; A.B.C.F.M. *Annual Report*, 1832, p. 66.
17. J. Tracey, *op. cit.*, p. 265; A.B.C.F.M. *Annual Report*, 1832, p. 66.

relationships being cordial Goodell and Dwight were invited to a very important event in the life of the Armenian Apostolic Church. The Peshtimaljian School, which was opened as a result of the "Farewell Letter," had trained a good number of young men, fifteen of whom sought ordination. The service was held on September 2, 1833, in which Goodell and Dwight participated, the former with a prayer.[18] During the ceremony an indiscreet incident endangered the relationship, but the situation was redeemed.[19]

In his 1835 correspondence, Goodell wrote that relations were of the "same pleasing character" with prospects for spiritual renovation to some extent, and that a high school had been opened by the mission with the "warm approbation of Peshtimaljian, principal of the Armenian Seminary."[20] Goodell reported as late as February 28, 1835, that he found scarcely any opposition from any quarter and his diary of April 2, 1835, recorded that "the good work goes on among the Armenians without any abatement. . . . Three of those who are most active in the reformation, and who talk and read and preach in all companies and on all occasions and with all boldness, are members of the great Synod by which everything relative to the affairs of the church or of the nation is regulated."[21] Even his notes of November 30, 1835, showed no sign of opposition, with "the good work among the Armenians," according to him, "steadily advancing from week to week, and it now seems to be carrying bishops, bankers, everything before it."[22]

Facts demonstrate, however, that there seems to have been hostility on the part of individual Armenians from the very beginning of the mission in Constantinople. Deroyentz Chamoorjian, an intellectual and lay church leader of the times, and a man with an autocratic spirit, is said to have objected strongly that Patriarch Garabed had received with honor in the

18. Prime, *op. cit.*, p. 159; *Missionary Herald*, February, 1834, p. 54; Dwight, *op. cit.*, pp. 40-41.

19. For this incident reference may be made to Yeghiayan, *op. cit.*, Chapter 9, pp. 4-6; Eutudjian, *op. cit.*, pp. 57-58. The reference is to the story that when the missionaries in the altar area were extended the Holy Bible so they could kiss it, Goodell and Dwight took it up, looked at it with the eyes of tourists, and after examining it said it was beautiful and gave it to the next person. Yeghiayan, recounting this incident, thinks it was rude and humiliating. Eutudjian, on the other hand, wrote that the missionaries made a tactical mistake. The demonstration of their "strong abhorence of the superstitious ceremonies might have led the ignorant and ritual-worshiping" public to abhor the missionaries and reduce their influence.

20. *Missionary Herald*, Vol. XXXII, January, 1836, p. 16.

21. Prime, *op. cit.*, pp. 178-181.

22. *Ibid.*, p. 186.

Church several American ministers.[23] Outside Constantinople, the reception was not the friendliest. When Smith and Dwight arrived at Etchmiadzin on November 19, 1830, they had a hostile reception from the monks who told their guide, Antonio, that the American missionaries were of the same school as the German missionaries at Shoosha who had come to convert the Armenians. The monks told the guide he was wrong in connecting himself with the Americans as he was in danger of imbibing their sentiments.[24] In Constantinople, a papal priest instigated a renowned Armenian jeweler to take two converts before Peshtimaljian [25] with the accusation they were in error and the Patriarch reproachfully commented to Goodell and Dwight during their attendance at a New Year service in the Armenian Church: "You will by and by, become a *preacher* to the Armenians."[26]

Up to 1836, however, opposition was chiefly by individuals. The hierarchy had not yet committed itself as antagonistic to the reform. [27] But with the opening of 1837, when the intention of the missionaries was more clearly evaluated, the authorities attempted to withdraw the Armenians from the influence of the missionaries. They did this by obtaining the sanctions of the bankers who were influential because of their riches and for being in favor before the Government as well as the governors and pashas. A resolution was passed by the council of the Armenian community to break up the High School. It was planned to do this "first by starting a large school in Hass Keuy, and then by ordering the parents of the students of the American High School to withdraw their children." [28]

The sporadic cases of opposition finally "culminated in 1839," according to Strong, "in an outbreak of vigorous persecution. The higher clergy had become frightened. As priests, they dreaded to lose any of their power over the people; as politicians they were suspicious of a movement which might disintegrate the ancient Church, now the only bond of the Armenian race."[29] Strong's judgment is perhaps biased. The clergy could conceivably have had nobler motives than the fear of the loss of power over

---

23. H.K. Murmurian, *Nineteenth Century and Hovhannes Deroyentz of Broosa* (Constantinople: 1908), pp. 46-47.

Of this visit Smith and Dwight say that the Patriarch made them to understand how much he loved them and was delighted by their visit. "In fact," they wrote, "we could with difficulty civilly avoid spending the night at his place." See Smith, Vol. I, *op. cit.*, p. 54. Smith and Dwight appear to be misinterpreting the Patriarch's oriental hospitality with the acceptance of their mission.

24. Smith, *op. cit.*, Vol. II, p. 95

25. *Missionary Herald*, Vol. XXXII, February, 1836, p. 41.

26. *Ibid.*, p. 47.

27. Dwight, *op. cit.*, p. 63.

28. *Ibid.*, pp. 66-67; Hamlin, *op. cit.*, pp. 65-66; Prime, *op. cit.*, p. 195.

29. Strong, *op. cit.*, p. 93.

the people. But, that the clergy were afraid the movement might disintegrate the ancient Church is a valid argument. In any case, Strong states it well when he says that there was an outbreak of persecution, though it may not be granted that it was "vigorous."

C. Causes for the Change

One important reason for the change of policy on the part of the Armenian Church is to be found in the "considerable headway" the evangelical movement had made—"so much headway, in fact," according to Arpee, "that the authorities of the church in their excitement estimated the evangelicals at about five hundred"[30] in 1838. Even as early as 1836, some had estimated that evangelicals amounted to 800. This was doubtless an enormous exaggeration.[31]

Evidences of the advance of evangelical work were seen in the establishment of a mission high school in Pera in the Lancastrian system,[32] the opening of a Girls' High School in Smyrna, the conducting of weekly Bible-study meetings and the commencement of a preaching ministry in Armenian, and the founding of the Society of the Pious.[33]

The mission had extended its influence, in addition, beyond Constantinople and Smyrna. A mission had been established in Broosa in 1834 under Benjamin Schneider, with a school in the city and a second one at Demir Tash six miles distant. Another mission had been established in Trebizond under Mr. Johnson.[34]

Even more importantly, the labors of the missionaries had been winning converts who were becoming vocal. Dwight wrote that the "Armenian brethren preach Christ, but occasionally, due to the nature of things, get into controversy."[35] To the conversion of Hovhannes Der Sahakian and Senekerim Der Minassian were added others among whom were: 1) Der Kevork, who became "an earnest preacher of the truth as it is in Jesus," and although never formally leaving the Armenian Church, exerted "a powerful influence in promoting the wonderful revival and work of true religion among his people" according to Goodell;[36] 2) Sarkis "varjabed," who, Goodell reports, renounced his errors and became "a useful assistant

30. Arpee, *A Century of Armenian Protestantism*, p. 10.
31. Tracey, *op. cit.*, p. 326.
32. *Missionary Herald*, Vol. XXXI, January, 1835, p. 7; Tracey, *op. cit.*, pp. 298, 309; Dwight, *op. cit.*, p. 44.
33 *Supra. Ch. 4. p. 44.*
34. Tracey, *op. cit.*, pp. 298-299.
35. *A.B.C.F.M. Annual Report*, 1845, p. 93.
36. Prime, *op. cit.*, pp. 159-160.

to the missionaries in the work of translation;"[37] 3) Apissoghom Khachadourian (Eutudjian), a cantor, who was to become the first Pastor of the Constantinople Armenian Evangelical Church, was converted; 4) in Nicomedia, two priests had been converted—Vertanes Yeznakian and Haroutune Baghdassarian;[38] 5) finally, there was Krikor Peshtimaljian[39]—learned,[40] liberal in views,[41] enlightened, well acquainted with Scripture, and deeply convinced of the errors of his church—who had a good deal of influence on Armenian affairs and was a friend of the missionaries.[42] In fact, Dwight states that all the converts "under the labours of the missionaries . . . and many of the later ones, were from among the alumni" of Peshtimaljian's school and "it is impossible to calculate the amount of influence exerted by Peshtimaljian, in preparing the minds of men to receive the true knowledge of the gospel."[43] At first he was alarmed at the boldness of his former pupils in advocating evangelical doctrines. But later he was convinced his pupils' interpretations of Scripture arose out of the very principles he had been inculcating. So he encouraged them privately, never publicly, and never had the option to decide one way or the other, as he died before the persecutions began.[44] Evidence shows that he did educate his pupils in evangelical ideas.[45] But, as with most events taking place during the period, there was also disagreement about Peshtimaljian's posture. Some considered him to be orthodox but that his name was exploited[46] by the missionaries to give the impression that Peshtimaljian was an adherent to protestant reformation views.[47]

37. Prime, *op. cit.*, p. 162.
38. The means of their conversion was a tract by Legh Richmond entitled "The Dairyman's Daughter." It was translated into Armeno-Turkish by Goodell in Malta, assisted by Bishop Dionysius who had also added a prayer at the end. The tract related the story of a young girl who had been converted but now lay dying. Her conversion was so genuine that she developed a concern for the salvation of her parents. Now this tract had been left, along with copies of "The Young Cottager," at the door of a Church in Nicomedia and it was carried to a priest by the boy who had received it. On reading and finding the way of salvation, the priest had given the news to the other priest of the village who also was similarly affected. They were affected so positively that they went to converse with the Patriarch to point out the need of "a revival of spiritual religion in the Armenian church." (See Prime, *op. cit.*, pp. 220-224; Tracey, *op. cit.*, p. 366).
39. Died on December 30, 1837 according to Berberian, *op. cit.*, p. 494.
40. Prime, *op. cit.*, p. 159; Tracey, *op. cit.*, p. 342.
41. Prime, *Ibid.*
42. Tracey, *op. cit.*, p. 279; *Missionary Herald*, 1836, February, p. 42.
43. Dwight, *op. cit.*, p. 27; Eutudjian, *op. cit.*, pp. 44-45.
44. Dwight, *op. cit.*, pp. 26-27.
45. Kassouny, *Loossashavigh*, pp. 23-24; *Missionary Herald*, Vol. XXX, Oct., 1834, p. 366.
46. Yeghiayan, *op. cit.*, Ch. 8, pp. 19-20. (In published work, pp. 189-190).
47. Those holding this view cite his book, *Loossashavigh* to demonstrate that Peshtimaljian's views defended the orthodox creed of the Armenian Church. They claim that in this work he recorded and explained the Nicene Creed and interpreted faith, the church, heresy, etc. without evidence of any deviations from the doctrines of the Armenian Church.
This argument is difficult to sustain for several reasons. First, it is to be noted that the first

A second important reason for the change of policy was the more definitive realization of the religious and theological intention of the missionaries—the realization also of differences in theological outlook. Avedis Berberian,[48] for instance, claimed that the missionaries in Constantinople were not honest with Patriarch Stepanos. "They showed themselves to be and made believe," he wrote, "that they were preachers to the Jews and the heathen, while at the same time praising the Armenians as being orthodox and true Christians. But at the end their falsehood was revealed. Not that they were working to bring the Jews and the heathen to the faith, but to mislead the Armenians so that they might accept their religion."[49] The theological posture of the missionaries came to be questioned. During an early visit by Goodell, Patriarch and vicar persisted with questions as to what kind of Christians the missionaries made their converts, what sect they followed, and what name they took.[50] During Goodell's second visit the vicar asked questions on funerals, priests, confession and the Eucharist to which the missionary answered reluctantly. Goodell's general answers to questions on the Eucharist didn't satisfy him. He asked for direct answers to the words of the institution, "This is my body," and "This is my blood." The question and answer, reported by Goodell, went like this:

Q. "Is it not, then, real flesh and blood that you partake of?"

A. "No; everybody among us knows better than that from the taste."

Q. "But do they not consider it to be changed?"

A. *"How* changed? Changed into *what*?"

Q. "Do they not, at least, suppose the power of God to be in it, in an especial manner?"

A. "When Christ says, 'I am the door,' and 'I am the vine,' is the power of God in the door or in the vine in a more special manner?

---

evangelicals were pupils of his school. Second, it must be remembered that the book was commissioned for writing by Patriarch Boghos for use in the Armenian Church and was completed in 1819. It was officially published as late as 1848, eleven years after Peshtimaljian's death. It might be counter-argued that the book, written in 1819, does not preclude the possibility that Peshtimaljian developed evangelical views about 1827, specially under the influence of King's "Farewell Letter." In truth, the book might have been published purposefully in 1848 to discredit Protestant statements to the effect that evangelical views were held by Peshtimaljian. (See Yeghiayan, *op. cit.*, Ch. 8, pp. 19-20). (In published work, pp. 189-190).

48. A historian contemporary to the events. He was the head of the council in the patriarchate—a kind of chamberlain.
49. Berberian, *op. cit.*, p. 295.
50. Prime. *op. cit.*, pp. 132-133; Eutudjian, *op. cit.*, pp. 49-50.

"Here all present burst into a hearty laugh, in which the vicar himself joined. He then asked whether I did not believe that there was something in it *essentially spiritual.* I replied that every bit and particle of it went into the stomach and was there digested, and was then 'cast out into the draught;' that the way to a man's heart was not through his mouth; that nothing entering in at the mouth goes to the heart, but to the stomach, and can neither purify nor 'defile the man' in any other sense except a physical one. Is it not so, Effendi?"

Q. "Yes, true; but is it, then, of no benefit to our *souls?*"

A. "Certainly; it was given us for no other purpose."

Q. "But if it be not *changed,* not made in some way *essentially holy,* how can it be of any *spiritual* benefit to us?"

A. "Are the letters of the alphabet *spiritual* substances, or *material,*— things made with men's hands?"

"The latter, certainly."

"But when we make use of these material things in reading the Scriptures, are not our souls benefited?"

"To this he, in the midst of another general laugh from those present, assented, and pressed me no more on the subject. . . . ."[51]

The hierarchy, on sensing the real difference between the views of their Church and of the missionaries, commenced to take a stricter stand in order to make sure that they defended the historic Church which had, over the centuries, withstood 'corrupting' influences. This concern may be considered to be an important cause for the change of attitude.

The third basic cause for the change of attitude, we believe, was the realization and observation that there could come about the disintegration of the unifying force of the Church. The Armenian amiras, therefore, as Kassouny believes, along with the hierarchy, "suspected that this new movement could undermine the Old Church, which was the only unifying element of the nation."[52] The Church hierarchy were even more conscious

51. Prime, *op. cit.*, pp. 138-140.
There are some important observations to be made. First of all, the interpretation of the Eucharist is a complex problem. The Armenian Church is literal on this issue. It also believes that salvation is imputed. Goodell on the other hand appears to be Zwinglian in his position when he interpretes the Eucharist to be a symbol and a remembrance, "not literal but figurative. . . ."
Second, it appears that Goodell failed to understand the subtlety of the laughter. It is conceivable that they were laughing at Goodell's inability or ignorance to understand the essential nature of the Eucharist and not at the humor of his argument.
52. Kassouny, *Loossashavigh*, p. 25.

of the fact that the Church was the common denominator stabilizing the social, intellectual and religious life of the nation. We concur with Wach that "Just as long as the various strata which make up society are united by some common denominator of interests or ideas major changes will not take place. Should this unifying force, however, be wholly or partly abrogated disintegration will take place to be followed by peaceful or bloody revolution."[53]. The great fear of the Armenian leadership was that the cementing force, the Church, might be weakened by a division in its body. The Church as well as the lay civic leaders were quite aware of the times in which they were living—a time of sudden changes in political power, a time of re-orientation of society—and as statesmen, if not sociologists, were conscious that the Protestant or evangelical-minded could become a sect in an effort of the community to integrate itself. For, as Wach aptly points out, "The sect is the effort of the whole community to integrate itself anew."[54]. There was enough of a commitment among sufficient numbers of Armenians to lead to the displacement of tradition, ritualism, and ceremonialism.

Due to these fears, the preference of the Armenian Church as well as those of the lay leaders was for national identity and national solidarity for "Through all these vicissitudes of national history the Armenian Church remained the only institution of any permanence among the Armenian people. It accompanied them wherever they went, from China to the British Isles, and from Alexandria to St. Petersburg, and proved, the Armenian language and literature not excepted, the most important bond of national unity. Thus, Armenian church and the Armenian people were more than ever closely identified."[55]

It can be understood therefore why the preference of the Church and the Armenians of influence was on the side of national solidarity rather than reform. In an effort, therefore, to be sympathetic to the woes of the Armenian Church, it should be stated that a tolerant or permissive attitude could have hardly been expected of the Armenian authorities. That would have been too much of an expectation. Even in progressive United States "religious liberty" was not easily granted by the churches. W.W. Sweet of the University of Chicago pointed out that religious freedom came as an economic factor when Baltimore and Pennsylvania, for instance, for economic as well as religious reasons advertised religious freedom in their chartered territories to draw settlers![56] Perry Miller of Harvard University claimed that Protestants stumbled into religious

53. Wach, *op. cit.*, p. 237.
54. *Ibid.*, p. 199.
55. Arpee, *The Armenian Awakening*, p. 10.
56. W.W. Sweet, "The American Colonial Environment and Religious Liberty." Church History, Volume IV, March, 1935, No. 1, pp. 43-56.

liberty—the Protestant churches did not so much achieve it as had liberty thrust upon them. In the article, "The Contribution of the Protestant Churches to Religious Liberty in Colonial America"[57] he argued that Protestant Churches considered toleration to be a dangerous and heathen notion, and strove to establish one official church in absolute uniformity. Protestant *intention* in America was not towards religious toleration, and that in their original intention, Protestants were intolerant.[58]

The Armenian Church likewise saw no advantage in toleration. On the contrary, it saw the destruction of its solidarity in it. Neither economic nor other factors were ever seen as advantages to be pursued. Consequently, when the Church finally saw the American mission was making incursions into its flock, and the lay leadership observed the inadequacies of religious enthusiasm as demonstrated by the converts, the situation was incendiary enough to give them the alarm to attempt to change the trend. It is true there were no Charles Chauncys among them to challenge the "revival" on intellectual grounds and write treatises similar to "Seasonable Thoughts."[59] But, they found the "enthusiasm" of the newly-converted disturbing and unacceptable.

Therefore, 1) *alarmed at the headway the American mission had made among Armenians,* 2) *doubtful of the theological position of the missionaries, and 3) fearful that the Protestant incursion would destroy the bond of union between Church and Nation* the combined lay and religious leadership *reacted negatively.* It is in the nature of things that the weak get frightened more easily than the strong; they also develop greater and deeper suspicions. Fear and suspicion lead to acts of defense. We believe that by 1839 fear and suspicion had reached a saturation point so as to lead the Church to change its attitude and to take steps to obstruct the new tide of conversions.

D. The First Round of Persecution—1839

On March 3, 1838, therefore, "all missionary publications were by patriarchal bull put under the ban, and all those who were in possession of heretical books were called upon to deliver them up to their spiritual overseers."[60] According to Eutudjian the bull prohibited the reading of the

---

57.   Perry G.E. Miller, *Church History,* March, 1935, pp. 57-66.
58.   *Ibid.*
59.   Charles Chauncy: "Seasonable Thoughts on the State of Religion in New England," 1743, written in opposition to Jonathan Edwards' "Some Thoughts concerning the Present Revival of Religion in New England," 1742.
60   Arpee, *A Century of Armenian Protestantism,* p. 11.

72

publications coming out of the William Griffith printing press of Smyrna, as well as the reading of the Holy Bible and the Gospel. It also instructed those who possessed such publications either to burn them themselves or to hand them over to the patriarchate for burning.[61] Apissoghom Khachadourian (Eutudjian), zealously holding to his father's traditions, burned all such possessions, considering it a service to God![62]

On April 28, 1839, *all* communication with the missionaries was prohibited by a new patriarchal bull, "more violent," according to Dwight, "than the former."[63] The bull threatened terrible anathemas against all who should be found having relationships with the missionaries, or reading their books; and also against all who neglected to inform when made acquainted with offenders.[64]

When opponents of the "Pietistic Union" and of the "Temperance Society" the Union had founded[65] attempted to destroy the "Pietistic Union," they faced the opposition of their own leader, Patriarch Stepan. He was popular with the people because of his humble nature, so the opposers found it difficult to enforce on him unacceptable procedures. Consequently, those in opposition, specially the influential Amiras, brought Bishop Hagopos Seropian, primate of Marsovan, as "Pokhanort" to Patriarch Stepan.[66] "Pokhanort" Hagopos Seropian entered the patriarchate on February 5, 1839.[67] He was a religious fanatic and extreme conservative. Two days after taking office, namely, on February 7, [68] 1839, Hagopos commenced a persecution of the evangelicals. He arrested suddenly "varjabeds" [69] Hovhannes Der Sahakian and Physica Boghos, kept them in prison for four days until an imperial firman for their exile was obtained, and despatched them to the St. Garabed monastery in Caesaria, 400 miles east of Constantinople.[70] Berberian, adding Hovhannes Yeznakian, Vartabed Tovmas and Der Kevork Ardzrouni to the list, says that they were sent "without examination of the accusation that they have become Lutherans."[71] Ormanian, listing all five, says that Hagopos' step "was a thoughtless one, for with the exception of Der Sahakian the others were neither Protestant nor favoring Protestantism

61. Eutudjian, *op. cit.,* pp. 98-99.
62. *Ibid.,* Prime, *op. cit.,* p. 233.
63. Dwight, *op. cit.,* p. 94.
64. *Ibid.*
65. Eutudjian, *op. cit.,* p. 91.
66. Eutudjian, *op. cit.,* p. 91; Ormanian, *op. cit.,* p. 3722; Prime, *op. cit.,* p. 323; Dwight, *op. cit.,* pp. 88-89.
67. Ormanian, *op. cit.,* p. 3722.
68. Goodell and Dwight give February 19, 1839.
69. Means teachers.
70. Eutudjian, *op. cit.,* p. 92; Prime, *op. cit.,* pp. 232-234; Ormanian, *op. cit.,* p. 3722; Dwight, *op. cit.,* p. 90.
71. Berberian, *op. cit.,* pp. 496-497.

but were following philosophical studies and wanted to benefit from those who had come from America."[72]

Patriarch Stepan tried to stop this "cruel strictness and persecution," [73] according to Eutudjian. But, unable to do so , he resigned and Hagopos became Patriarch immediately on March 13, 1839. Hagopos' first act as Patriarch was to exile priest Der Kevork Ardzrouni on March 14, 1839,[74] with two other "vartabeds" after imprisoning them for about a month, and a little later Mesrob "varjabed" Taghiantyantz of Erivan for siding with those who wanted reformation.[75] The latter, according to Eutudjian, managed to get away by tricks to India instead of being exiled to Siberia as planned.[76]

Others were called up, whom Goodell puts at some five hundred, "including bishops, priests, bankers, and c., who were to be examined about their evangelical views." [77]

The persecution was also directed against the missionaries, who were formally accused before the Turkish authorities of having made proselytes from the Armenians, an offence against the Sublime Porte. A strong influence was brought to bear upon the government to secure their banishment from the country, "their aim being," according to Goodell, "nothing less than to effect our entire removal from the country." [78] Dwight enlarged on this thought when he wrote that the imperial bankers, who had been dispossessed of their power by being replaced by the artisan class in Armenian affairs and by the Sultan's chief architect and the superintendent of the Government powder works, labored for "the expulsion of Protestantism." The expulsion of the missionaries became a project. They were represented to the Sultan as being rebellious against the government of the Patriarch—an accusation which was practically equivalent to being rebellious to the Sultan's government. In addition, a fabricated[79] charge was presented that "a book in Turkish, authored by the missionaries, had attacked the Mohammedan religion."[80] Hamlin, on the same issue, presented the view that the Greek Orthodox and the Caliph of Islam joined the Armenian efforts to expel the missionaries. He wrote that to the anathema of the Armenian Church was added that of the Oriental Orthodox Greek Church, and the Caliph of Islam joined his voice with a message enjoining the Christian shepherds to look well after their

72. Ormanian, *op. cit.*, p. 3722.
73. Eutudjian, *op. cit.*, p. 93.
74. Dwight, *op. cit.*, p. 93; Prime, *op. cit.*, p. 233.
75. Eutudjian, *op. cit.*, p. 94.
76. *Ibid.*, pp. 93-98. Cyrus Hamlin, *Among the Turks* (New York: American Tract Society, 1877), pp. 32-37.
77. Prime, *op. cit.*, p. 234.
78. Prime, *op. cit.*, p. 236.
79. According to missionary Dwight.
80. Dwight, *op. cit.*, pp. 85-87.

flocks. Then, with German De Boutineff's counsel, an order was obtained from Sultan Mahmud to expel all the missionaries. The situation was saved, according to Hamlin, when American Commodore Porter consulted his government and his government replied, soon after the death of Mahmud on July 1, 1839, that the American missionaries must be accorded the same protection as the papal missionaries.[81]

Strong sums up the whole commencement of the first round of persecutions in these words:

> The tolerant patriarch was replaced; a list of those suspected of heresy was said to contain the names of 500 prominent persons, bishops, priests, and bankers. Arrests were made and terror spread. Repeated pronouncements by both Greek and Armenian ecclesiastics denounced the missionaries as 'Satanic heresiarchs from the caverns of hell and the abyss of the northern ocean.' Schools were broken up; the press was silenced; books were burned in bonfires upon city squares. A systematic effort to expel the missionaries was likely to have succeeded had not war broken out between the pasha of Egypt and the sultan, which terminated in the defeat and death of the latter, and stayed the persecution.[82]

It is this researcher's feeling that the Armenians could not have remained silent and inactive against the activities of the missionaries who were establishing a bridgehead in the nation. If they had remained silent, they would have come under the judgment of Armenian historians. Therefore, their reaction was legitimate, and under the "illiberal" traditions of the period, unavoidable. Though legitimate, it does not mean, however, that the reaction was wise for it was easily interpretable as a form of persecution.

E. Temporary Discontinuance of Persecution

The sudden reaction against the missionaries which commenced in the

---

81. Hamlin, *op. cit.*, pp. 37-40.
82. Strong, *op. cit.*, p. 93.
    Strong's use of the words "stayed the persecution" may be overdrawn. The Armenian Church refuses to accept that the actions taken against certain dissenting Armenians was persecution. The action of the Armenian Church against the missionaries through governmental intervention is either denied or explained as necessary to block the subterfuge of the missionaries. In a sense, it is to be agreed that the Armenian Church authorities were not doing anything that was not within the jurisdiction of the Patriarch. Legally, as will be seen in greater detail in Chapter 9, the Patriarch was the protector of Armenian Orthodoxy and the civil rights of his people. The priests and teachers in the national schools were appointed by the Armenian Church through its regular lay councils. Therefore, any action of discipline was a legitimate expression of the Patriarch's authority. Transference of priests and teachers from one area to another, was explained as disciplinary action.

early part of 1839 was equally suddenly reversed by early July of the same year. It may be worthwhile to investigate the reason for the discontinuance of the "persecution" which was to be resumed in 1844.

Dwight credited Providence for the stoppage. He saw the hand of God in the sudden death of the Sultan "who was aiding the persecutors."[83] He also believed that God brought on the death of the wife of one of the persecutors, and meted out suffering to another powerful man "who had more than once, or twice, actively opposed and persecuted the evangelical brethren." Speaking of that "powerful" man he said that "within a short space of time he lost two daughters by sudden death; a third daughter became deranged, and also a daughter-in-law; his wife was deformed by sickness, and also made nearly blind, and he himself became a miserable invalid."[84] This attitude is about as superstitious as that of the adherents of the Armenian Church whose proponent, Berberian, claimed that the anathema of Matteos Patriarch of 1845 on seven of the leaders[85] resulted in paying for their apostasy by serious illness.[86] If Dwight will quote Providence, Berberian will meet him with the same measure.

But, these and other historians have given better reasons. In 1839 the war with Mohammed Ali of Egypt was renewed. This event forced Sultan Mahmoud to demand from the several Patriarchs, among whom was the Armenian Patriarch, to furnish recruits for the army, thus shifting the attention of the Armenians from the missionaries to a more vital question.[87] On June 24, 1839, a Turkish army of 80,000 were routed by the Egyptians.[88] Before news of this disaster reached Sultan Mahmoud, he died on July 1, 1839, and was replaced by his 16-year old son, Abdul Medjid.[89] On July 11, 1839, the ceremony of the girding of the sword was inaugurated, placing the young Sultan on the throne officially.[90] The consequences of his accession were several: The Armenian bankers of influence in the government, through money they lent to the pashas, lost their wealth; the old Patriarch Stepan, who was friendly to the missionaries and evangelicals, was reinstated and Hagopos dismissed; about the middle of August, 1839, the Armenian Synod convened and resolved to recall the exiles from banishment, except Der Sahakian who was considered to be the ringleader of the sect called "Evangelicals."[91]

83. Dwight, *op. cit.*, p. 105.
84. *Ibid.*
85. Der Sahakian and his early followers.
86. Berberian, *op. cit.*, pp. 303-304.
87. Prime, *op. cit.*, p. 237; Tracey, *op. cit.*, p. 388.
88. Prime, *op. cit.*, p. 238; Dwight, *op. cit.*, p. 96.
89. Berberian, *op. cit.*, p. 498; Eutudjian, *op. cit.*, p. 100; Dwight, *op. cit.*, p. 96; Prime, *op. cit.*, p. 238.
90. Prime, *op. cit.*, p. 238; Tracey, *op. cit.*, p. 388.
91. Prime, *op. cit.*, p. 239; Tracey, *op. cit.*, p. 389; Dwight, *op. cit.*, pp. 96-99; Eutudjian, *op. cit.*, p. 100.

Der Sahakian was finally to be brought back through the mediation of the Sultan's sister on request from her English physician. As a result, on November 14, 1839, an imperial request to the Patriarch brought him back.[92]

On November 3, 1839, in the presence of religious heads and foreign ambassadors, Abdul Medjid had his vizier read the first formal Bill of Rights, the Magna Carta of Turkey called in Turkish "Hatti Sherif of Gul Hane."[93] Since, among other things, the Hatti Sherif guaranteed security of "life, honor, and property"[94] the suppression of the Armenian dissidents became politically inexpedient.

Thus, the defeat of the 80,000-man army by Mohammed Ali of Egypt on June 24, 1839; Mahmoud's death on July 1, 1839; and the accession of Abdul Medjid to the throne stopped the persecutions and led the Armenian Synod to recall Patriarch Stepan and the exiles.[95] And, "The evangelistic work was resumed with new courage,"[96] with the former usurping Patriarch Hagopos saying, "At heart I was against the persecutions that took place, but I did them on the enforcement of the Amiras."[97]

It has been demonstrated amply that the Armenian Church, while at first it accommodated the missionaries because it was not quite aware of the basic direction of the American mission work among Armenians, changed its attitude towards them very distinctly by 1839. The basic cause for the change was the Church's realization that the missionaries were preaching doctrines unacceptable to the Armenian Church and it feared that the incursion would destroy the national identity and solidarity of its people. As a result, the Armenian Church, goaded by the lay leadership, used all of its legitimate obstructive procedures to nullify the work of the American missionaries. But, circumstances so brought it about that the Armenian Church was unable to continue its policy of opposition openly. As a result, instead of obstructing the work of the American Board, they unwittingly paved the way for more open and stronger endeavors by the missionaries and their converts. In other words, the policy of coercion failed to block American missionary progress among the Armenians. It created a situation which led to greater polarization, as the more statesmanlike Patriarch Stepan had rightly stated it would happen—that "strictness brings about contrary results."[98]

---

92. Dwight, *op. cit.*, pp. 96-99.
93. Prime, *op. cit.*, pp. 240-241.
94. *Ibid.*
95. Dwight, *op. cit.*, pp. 96-99.
96. Hamlin, *op. cit.*, p. 40.
97. Eutudjian, *op. cit.*, p. 101.
98. Ormanian, *Azkabadoum*, Col. 2541, p. 3721.

CHAPTER VII

THE FINAL SEPARATION

A. *The Second Round of Persecution*

The second round of persecutions began lightly with the ascension to the patriarchal throne of Matteos Choohajian on July 13, 1844 and in serious earnestness in early 1846. On his ascension to the throne, there were ten reasons why persecution against the Protestants was unavoidable.[1] He began to apply restraining measures towards the end of 1844[2] but really intensified his efforts in early 1846.[3]

Berberian, speaking of the strategy of the missionaries, accuses them of entering Armenian homes pretending to be friends and trying to attract the simple-minded and "catch them in their claws;" to help the poor and debtors and to provide money to win them; to establish free schools and give "the poison of their false teaching" along with other learning.[4] This eyewitness lists ten of the teachings of the missionaries which opposed the Armenian Church's teachings. First of all, he writes, they declared that there was no other book other than the Gospel.[5] Second, they stated that the church of Christ is invisible; that there is no visible church. Third, they rejected the mysteries of the church. Fourth, they refused to accept the transubstantiation[6] of the bread and wine used at Mass into the body and blood of Christ. Fifth, they denied the mediation of the saints; sixth, the

---

1. Kevork-Mesrob, *History of the Armenian Church,* pp. 518-519.

Kevork-Mesrob lists eight reasons for the rise of persecution against the Protestants, namely, 1) the Armenian Catholic conflict and the spiritual condition it created among Armenians; 2) the fanatical zeal of the patriarchs, lay leadership, and the clergy; 3) the fanatical zeal of the Amiras who became cause for inciting the clergy; 4) the example of the sister communities, such as that of the Greek Orthodox; 5) the encouragement of the Imperial Government; 6) the competing interests of the European nations; 7) the extreme positions of the missionaries and the newly-converted Armenian Protestants; and 8) the dark ignorance of the greater class of the Armenian Community. But, there were two additional and more fundamental reasons. One was that the Protestant movement had grown even stronger, and the other, that theological differences had become more clearly apparent.

2. Dwight, *op. cit.,* p. 171; Strong, *op. cit.,* p. 104; Prime, *op. cit.,* p. 303.

3. Prime, *op. cit.,* p. 307.

4. Berberian, *op. cit.,* p. 296.

5. Evangelion, translated into Armenian as "Avedaran" or the "Book of the Good News." Berberian points out that for this reason the Evangelicals called themselves "Avedaranagan" (Evangelical).

6. Berberian and Deroyentz both use the Armenian word "KOYAPOKHOUTUNE" for transubstantiation, which is a parallel meaning. But, Armenian Church theologians today use "POKHARGOUTUNE" in order to demonstrate their divergence from the Roman Catholic position.

virginity of the Mother of God until her ascension; seventh, the confession of sins to the high priest; eighth, the worshiping of the cross; ninth, the veneration of the pictures of saints; and tenth, fasting and other canons of the Church.[7]

The Patriarch's first effort was to use friendly persuasion as a bait to win the *evangelical leaders* over.[8] The best instance of this policy was Choohajian's attempt to win back to the Mother Church Apissoghom Khachadoorian (Eutudjian), to whom, according to Dwight and Eutudjian, the Patriarch[9] offered a larger salary than what the missionaries were giving in exchange for going over to the Patriarch's side and, while retaining his own private convictions, keeping silent and not speaking his sentiments to others.[10] When kindliness and friendliness as a policy failed to bring results with the leaders, the policy of fatherly pursuasion was applied on a larger scale to the public. Desirous of knowing the number of the "prodigals" in the nation who had followed the "unclean sect" he had the church records checked in Constantinople and the surroundings and found that there were eight thousand of them. He had the priests speak to many and he himself invited many of the "prodigals" who had swerved from the truth and spoke to them respectfully and asked them why they had departed from the bosom of the mother church and followed a false religion.[11] Berberian continues to report that the Patriarch found that many, due to poverty, had been deceived by payment of money, some receiving salaries. He promised to give them stipends, and they went to their priests, confessed and asked pardon. In this way, the number of the 'lost' was reduced to three thousand.[12] And, those who had been deceived on account of their simplemindedness that the mediation of the saints and the veneration of icons were idol worship, were convinced by the sermons of the Patriarch which were given in many churches on Sunday afternoons.

In the meantime, a subtle economic pressure was placed upon those who had not turned back to the Mother Church. According to the civil law, shopkeepers and artisans were dependent upon patrons. The Patriarch secretly directed the patrons to withdraw their patronage, according to Dwight and Goodell, leaving the Evangelical shopkeepers

---

7. Berberian, *op. cit.*, p. 296.
8. Eutudjian, *op. cit.*, pp. 128-129; Dwight, *op. cit.*, p. 175.
9. Kevork-Mesrob informs us in a footnote on p. 516 in the book mentioned earlier that on the day of his resignation on April 1, 1848, Patriarch Matteos announced to the Church Council that he had personally spent 37,865 piastres to stop the growth of protestantism.
10. Dwight, *op. cit.*, pp. 230-231; Dwight, *Christianity Revived*, pp. 199-201; Anderson, *op. cit.*, pp. 398-400.
11. Berberian, *op. cit.*, p. 297; Yeghiayan, *op. cit.*, Chapter 10, p. 11. (In published work, p. 241.)
12. Berberian, *op. cit.*, p. 297.

without business. He also ordered the priests to give him the names of those who did not go to confession.[13] The aim was to wear out the patience of the Evangelicals by depriving them of their income and thus reducing them to submission.[14] This economic persecution, which was to be practised more intensely in 1846, was hitting at the most vulnerable point because the victim was being left without a civil status.[15]

More drastic measures followed in the ensuing months when it became evident that the movement could not be arrested entirely.

B. Debates and Public Discourses

The Patriarch turned next to debates and public discourses on religious topics in order to demonstrate the correctness of the teachings and services of the Armenian Church in order to win back the dissidents.[16]

The first debate was held in the home of cantor Hovhannes Mehendizian in Constantinople. Those in attendance agreed that Apissoghom Khachadoorian (Eutudjian) would speak on behalf of the Society of the Pious and Badveli[17] Deroyentz (Chamoorjian) put forward important questions. He wanted to know what proof Eutudjian had to show that the Bible was the revelation of God; what the mysteries of the Church were; why each Christian should feel obliged to read the Holy Bible on his own and understand it; what Baptism and Communion were.[18] Deroyentz would not grant individual interpretation of the Bible, delegating that responsibility to the Church so that error might be avoided. He claimed Baptism was necessary for wiping out original sin, and Communion was the act of partaking of the real body and blood of Christ.[19] Eutudjian could not grant recognition to the interpretations given, arguing that the Bible was simple enough to speak to the individual reader. Baptism he received

13. Dwight, *op. cit.*, pp. 171-175.
14. Prime, *op. cit.*, p. 303.
15. (This question will be treated in greater detail in Chapter 9 of this work.)
16. Dwight believes that these debates were organized by the Patriarch in order to destroy the influence of Apissoghom Khachadoorian (Eutudjian). The Protestants were challenged to send their strongest man to meet the famous champion of orthodoxy, Hovhannes Deroyentz (Chamoorjian). The arrangements for the meetings were such as to favor the Patriarch's party, the sessions being held in the homes of men of their own thinking and the subjects for discussion being selected by the advocates of the Church and concealed from the Protestants by design. (See Dwight, *op. cit.*, pp. 179-180).
17. An Armenian word which means "one to be honored" or "honorable" and was used as a title for teachers in those days. At the present, the term is used for Protestant ministers.
18. Dwight, *op. cit.*, pp. 179-180.
19. Yeghiayan and others have suggested that Deroyentz had Roman Catholic training and leanings.

as the symbol whereby one dies unto sin and Communion as the act of remembrance of Christ. This first meeting lasted nine hours.

The second meeting was held in Hass Keuy in the home of Amira Nigoghos Nevrouzian with more than forty in attendance. Eutudjian pressed that the Old and New Testaments, as God's message, be recognized as final arbiter, but Chamoorjian would not grant it. Between April and June of 1845, six such meetings were held. In the last meeting Chamoorjian persisted in his argument that Christians are obliged to learn their faith and their doctrines from the Church, while Apissoghom Eutudjian established the Biblical position that faith comes as a result of obedience to the words of Christ. [20]

Patriarch Matteos Choohajian and his colleagues, according to Dwight, noted that instead of serving their ends, the meetings were bringing the opposite results. At least Dwight believed that the simple Scriptural arguments of Eutudjian had more effect on the minds of those present than the scholastic logic and learning of the antagonist. [21] Consequently, the Patriarch prohibited their continuation.

In place of the debates in residences, the Patriarch and his advisors organized public sessions in the patriarchal complex. [22] The discourses had as purpose the resolution of doubts and the series was entitled, "Loodzeech Daragoossanatz." [23] The purpose of these public sessions was to enlighten those who were in doubt and to influence them to accept the validity of the teachings of the Apostolic Church of Armenia. The technique was similar to that of the missionaries who had, through publicity, convinced many Armenians to believe in their kind of teaching. [24]

During the second of the public meetings at the patriarchal room in June, two important topics were taken up, viz., "Faith and Works" and "The Infallibility of the Church." Badveli Deroyentz lectured at length to demonstrate the necessity of works for salvation, and, the infallibility of the Church as the depository of doctrinal truth given to it through the centuries. These public sessions were open to the faithful members of the Church, but attendance by Evangelicals was not prohibited. Therefore, two Evangelicals who were present obtained permission to speak. Stepan Seropian [25] demonstrated from the Scriptures that "salvation is through faith" and that "it is a free grace which comes to the sinful Christian

20. Eutudjian, *op. cit.,* p. 132.
21. Dwight, *op. cit.,* pp. 179 f.
22. Berberian, *op. cit.,* p. 297; Yeghiayan, *op. cit.,* Ch. 10, p. 11. (In published work, p. 241.)
23. May be translated "Solution of Doubts."
24. Yeghiayan, *op. cit.,* Chapter X, p. 11. (In published work, p. 241.)
25. The brother of Patriarch Hagopos who had persecuted the Evangelicals.

through the living and true faith he has in Christ. This faith becomes a spring for good works in him. Thus good works result from faith and are not the cause for salvation." [26] Against the Roman position of the infallibility of the Church, schoolteacher Avedis Hussian took a stand. He said: "Infallibility belongs to God alone. Because the Church is a body composed of fallible men, it is necessary, for that very reason, that infallibility rest on the infallible word of God so that the Church might be secure. Otherwise, it can fall into many errors." [27] Evangelical authors, perhaps boastfully, claim that Deroyentz was left without an answer and the crowd with one voice favored the interpretation of the Evangelicals. [28]

C. Patriarch Choohajian's Paper of Recantation and New Creed

The Patriarch took a more concrete step next, and asked those in doubtful standing in the Armenian Church to sign a paper of repentance.

Called the "Paper of Recantation" [29] this document was written at the patriarchate from the mouth of those who were to recant and was addressed to the Patriarch. It was a good tool to bring back to the bosom of the Armenian Church those not fully convinced of its errors, but it was too humiliating for those who were so convinced and could only arouse the ire of the "reformed."

The person to sign it was to confess that he was born in the holy and spotless Christian religion and nourished in the Catholic doctrines of the holy Armenian Church. But, he was deceived "by the wicked enticements of Satan . . . and caught in the loose and soul-destroying doctrines of the New Sectaries." He was further to acknowledge that he had lovingly joined "this impious sect . . . and wilfully remained obstinate in error," but that after the counsel of the Patriarch as highpriest the "bands of our soul were broken, and the stupor which reigned over our hearts, dispelled . . . and became aware that what we had done was against the Divine power . . . and that the preaching of *those deceiving* New Sectaries . . . was nothing but an invention of arrogance, a snare of Satan, a sect of confusion, a

26. Eutudjian, *op. cit.,* p. 133.
27. *Ibid.,* p. 134.
28. *Ibid.* (This latter statement is perhaps an exaggeration, because if the discourses had carried the public with them, many more should have taken an evangelical stand—which is not the case.)
29. For Armenian, see Eutudjian, *op. cit.,* pp. 153-155; for English translation from the Armenian, see Dwight, *op. cit.,* pp. 327-329; in this work, see Appendix: "Paper of Recantation."

broad road which leadeth to destruction." As a result he was to repent, receive the spiritual and Christian authority of the Patriarch as Mediator, perform whatever penance was imposed, and confess that "the faith of the holy Church is spotless, her sacraments Divine, her rites of apostolic origin, her ritual pious." The one signing had also to accept *spiritual and temporal* punishment if he would return to his former impious way.

The intimidation that the paper bore was the wrong prescription for the "awakened." Because it did not resolve the problem entirely and because the Patriarch was unsatisfied with the indefiniteness of the "Paper of Recantation," he spelled out in detail the position of the Armenian Church in his "New Creed."[30] The New Creed's nine articles were presented for signature to the repentant as a sign of Orthodoxy. The document spelled out beliefs which were part and parcel of the practice of the Armenian Church, but which had not been presented as a formal creed at any time in its history. The repentant had to confess to the following: 1) that faith alone cannot save man, but that good works and confession in accordance with the belief of the universal church were necessary; 2) that the Church Militant, the visible church, has not and cannot err, and that there is no Scriptural truth that it does not acknowledge; 3) that it has seven sacraments which must be administered by a regularly ordained clergy who has received that authority from Christ through ordination; 4) that without baptism, one has no salvation even if he has not sinned at all; likewise, one cannot receive forgiveness of sins without confession of sins and repentance before a priest; 5) that the mystery of Holy Communion is the true body and blood of Christ and the one who does not partake of it is under eternal condemnation; 6) that the Holy Virgin Mary, the mother of God, kept her virginity both at the time of Christ's birth and afterwards; that she is worthy of honor above all saints; that the cross is worthy of adoration; that the relics and pictures of saints are worthy of honor through which God works miracles; 7) that to believe in the Church means to believe those things which the universal Church unitedly believes and that her external ceremonies and Christian rites have been received by tradition from the holy apostles and the holy fathers who succeeded them; 8) that in the Holy Church there are grades of authority, with the catholicoses and patriarchs as Christ's viceregents, and whose viciousness does not make the Church to err; 9) that those who preach that error has entered into the Holy Church must be anathematized; that such persons are "impious blasphemers of the Holy Spirit, and enemies of God and all his saints." Having thus confessed, he was to sign that he believed "the Holy Catholic Church of Christ is the

30. For the Armenian of Choohajian's New Creed, see Eutudjian, *op. cit.,* pp. 156-159; for the English translation, see Dwight, *op. cit.,* pp. 329-331; in this work, see Appendix: "The Patriarch's 'New Creed.' "

only pillar and ground of the truth, and whoever is out of the Church is not an heir of salvation."[31]

D. Protestant (Evangelical) Reaction

Between January 22 and July 1, 1846, the Armenian Evangelicals responded with three separate documents. When placed side by side with the "Paper of Recantation" and the "New Creed," they give conspicuous evidence that the two groups were locked in for a serious battle.

The first of these three documents is a letter written to the Patriarch by the membership of the Society of the Pious on January 22, 1846.[32] It was written three days before the first decree of Excommunication was issued on January 25, 1846.[33] The letter was signed, "Persecuted Christians," and was a protest against the "persecution, privation, accusation, and losses suffered by them." Pointing out that they had no one to go to but their nation which refuses to accept them as church members, they claimed they were orthodox and presented their doctrinal position. They affirmed that they believed: 1) in the Holy Trinity and in the Unity of Father, Son, and Holy Spirit; 2) in the Lord Jesus Christ, perfect man and perfect God, the only Saviour and mediator of believers; 3) in the Holy Spirit which is perfect God and source of truth; 4) in the Old and New Testament Scriptures which are the perfect rule of the Church; 5) in Baptism and Communion. They stated that if the Patriarch would like to investigate their faith further, he would find that their faith was the same as that accepted by the Church and taught by the Holy Gospel and that they accepted the Nicene Creed. They insisted that their faith was that which is taught in the Holy Scriptures, and that they cannot therefore accept "those demands" which are against Holy Writ and which are condemned in Scripture.[34] Stating further that they are Armenian by race, Christian by faith, and loyal subjects of the Empire they asked that they be pointed out their error as they cannot "work against their conscience before God." They pleaded that they be saved from their troubles and tribulations.[35]

The patriarchate reacted strongly and published on January 31, 1846, [36] or about nine days after the protest of the "Persecuted Christians," a 47-

---

31. *Ibid.*
32. Old School Calendar, January 9, 1846.
33. Old School Calendar, January 12, 1846.
34. Gal.1:8,9.
35. Eutudjian, *op. cit.*, pp. 160-162.
36. Old School Calendar, January 18, 1846.

page [37] booklet as an answer to the protesters. It is unlikely that this booklet reached the hands of the Evangelicals before the second decree of excommunication on February 1, 1846. [38] This important document made a rigid, unyielding, and uncompromising statement about the position of the Armenian Church, beginning with the statement that individuals from among the Armenian nation call themselves persecuted, when there is no persecutor in reality. It claimed the Church was only admonishing the errants, and not persecuting; it pointed out the evangelicals were contradicting Scripture and that it was the responsibility of the Patriarch, the shepherd of the flock, to reform the incorrigible by informing the children of the Church that they should be careful not to associate with such persons and not read their books so that they might not be deceived by their errant doctrines. What has the Patriarch done, by cautioning the people in this way, to cause them to say they are persecuted? When he protects the faithful that Christ has given to his care, does that mean it is persecuting others? When he locks the doors and the windows to prevent the thief from entering, does that mean he is persecuting the thief? Let it be stated, therefore, that the new sectaries have no right at all to call themselves persecuted. Not only is there no one persecuting them, but there is no one stopping them from speaking. They can talk among themselves whatever they want. The holy Patriarch is only ordering the pious and faithful people to shut their ears against such persons and not to read their books for fear they might lose their simplicity. The proclamation continued to instruct that it is not sufficient to read the Holy Bible to have faith without a guide; that the Church of Armenia is the faithful depository of the beliefs Gregory the Illuminator preached; that the faithful should learn their doctrines from the books of the holy Church and pray to God that the light that enlightened the Holy Loossavorich [39] may enlighten their minds also; that they should never ask for another spirit, because then the spirit of error would rule them. [40]

The second Evangelical Document is the proclamation addressed to the public by the newly-founded Church giving reasons or justifications for the separation. [41] Addressing themselves to the nation, they first presented their beliefs. They believed the Christian Church to be a spiritual covenant established by Christ with the purpose of keeping Godliness alive, keeping His holy day, preaching the Gospel and teaching men all Christian virtues

37. Patriarchate. "Proclamation One." (Constantinople: Muhendissian Press), 1846, pp. 1-47.
38. Old School Calendar, January 19, 1846.
39. Reference is to Gregory the Illuminator, Loossavorich meaning "illuminator." "Illuminator father" is also spoken of Gregory, the founder of the Armenian Church.
40. Patriarchate, "Proclamation One," op. cit., pp. 1-47; Yeghiayan, op. cit., Chapter 11, pp. 21-24. (In published work, pp. 253-255).
41. Eutudjian, op. cit., pp. 169-73.

and preparing their souls for heaven. They believed the Old and New Testaments to be the Church's only infallible and perfect canon and they considered it to be the responsibility of every Christian to accept the Bible as the guide of his faith and conduct. They claimed that it was in obedience to the Gospel that they "refused and put aside all those man-made traditions, rites and ceremonies, which are contrary to the Gospel and the purity and reformation of the Christian Church, which the Patriarch of our nation demanded that we accept."[42] They informed the nation that they had had no intention of separating from the Church whose members they were, but that, a New Creed was forced illegally upon them in 1846 in that the Armenian Church has no other Creed except the Nicene in which, they said, they believed. This New Creed, composed of nine articles, in its ninth one anathemized those who preached against the worship of the cross, relics and pictures of saints. Therefore, "more obedient to God rather than men" they did not accept the New Creed. As a result, they persisted, "the Church persecuted us by publicly reading anathemas against us."[43] They therefore considered it impossible to be reunited with the Church since they could not re-enter it without accepting those aberrations which had entered the Church in the course of centuries. This situation justified them to establish the *Evangelical Church of Armenia.*[44] They concluded by saying that because Patriarch Matteos Choohajian had used his entire ability and authority to destroy Evangelicalism and had tried to deprive them of the mysteries of the Church; because they felt responsible to their families and children to teach them the precepts of Jehovah, which could not be done without the public preaching of the Gospel; because Christ is the head of the Church and they had accepted His holy teachings and obeyed the Gospel sincerely; and because the holy Gospel commands all men to pray for all men and specially for kings and all leaders—they felt that they were not only "justified" but were "obliged" to found a separate Church.[45]

The third Document is a twelve-article Confession of Faith of the newly-established Church,[46] in which the church member states he believes as follows: 1) that there is only one living and true God who is the only proper object of worship; 2) that God exists in three persons of Father, Son and Holy Spirit and that these are one God; 3) that the Holy Scriptures, given by the inspiration of God, are the sufficient and only rule of faith and

42. *Ibid.*, p. 169.
43. *Ibid.*, p. 171.
44. This was the name given to the Evangelical Church in the beginning, which was later, through usage, called Armenian Evangelical Church.
45. Eutudjian, *op. cit.*, pp. 169-172.
46. For the Confession of Faith, see Dwight, *op. cit.*, pp. 336-338; *A.B.C.F.M., Annual Report,* 1846, pp. 239-240; in this work, see Appendix: "Confession of Faith of the Evangelical Church of Armenia."

practice; 4) that man in his natural state is destitute of holiness and justly exposed to the wrath of God; 5) that Jesus Christ is the only Saviour of sinners and the only mediator and intercessor between God and man; 6) that because of the depravity of man, it is necessary that all should be regenerated by the power of the Holy Ghost in order to be saved; 7) that man is justified by faith alone and not by any fastings, alms, penances, or other deeds of our own and that good works cannot be meritorious ground of salvation; 8) that conscientious discharge of duties to God, men and self are essential to the constructing of Christian character; 9) that worship must be offered through no other mediation than that of Jesus Christ alone and that the use of relics, pictures, crosses, and images is directly contrary to the Scriptures; 10) that at the resurrection from the dead the punishment of the wicked will commence at death and continue without end; 11) that any number of believers duly organized constitute a church of Christ, with Christ as the Head, and the sacraments of Baptism and the Lord's Supper as the only valid ones; 12) that the Gospel is the true and chief instrument appointed by Christ for the conversion of men and that it is the duty of Christ's Church to preach that Gospel to every creature. [47]

These three Evangelical Documents, namely, "The Persecuted Christians," the "Declaration of Reasons for Organized Protestant Churches," and the "Confession of Faith" were formulated over a period of at least six months. Both the missionaries as well as the "awakened" had anticipated the probability of such a turn of events, and had thought out carefully their doctrinal and disciplinary position. On reviewing these three documents, it will be observed that Patriarch Matteos Choohajian's "New Creed" is refuted and challenged fundamentally. [48]

The Protestant documents actually challenged practically everything that the Armenian Church held dear. Its rites and ceremonies were condemned as erroneous. Its belief that the faithful found salvation through the sacraments and rites of the Church, was cast out. Its right to the interpretation of the Scriptures, in the light of the Bible and traditions, was stripped and given to the individual Christian. It is evident that matters now have reached a point in which the question is not one of attempting to enlighten the Armenian Apostolic Church and the Armenian nation, and bring an internal reformation. It is rather a veritable Protestant Reformation that is being asked. The claim is that salvation is by faith alone, that the Bible is the only guide for faith and conduct, and the individual is capable of interpreting Scripture through the guidance of the Holy Spirit. Therefore, the answer to the missionaries and the

47. Appendix: "Confession of Faith of the Evangelical Church of Armenia."
48. For a tabulated summary of the "New Creed" and the Protestant point of view see Appendix: "Comparison of the Theological Positions of the Two Groups."

Armenian Evangelical position was "Voch."[49] Plainly, *the Church of Gregory the Illuminator was saying that the new Evangelical "converts" were heretics; and the Evangelicals were saying that the Holy Apostolic Church of Armenia was neither holy nor Apostolic and needed reformation and purification. The cup was full.*

E. Excommunication Decrees

We shall retrace our steps to the beginning of 1846. The Patriarch instructed that his decree of excommunication[50] be read in all the churches on January 25,[51] 1846. On the occasion of the reading, the great veil of the patriarchal church in Constantinople was drawn in front of the altar, after the church was darkened, and the anathema was solemnly read against priest Vertanes.[52]

There was an immediate reason for the excommunication, however, as Berberian relates. As it so often occurs in history the basic reason was drowned out by the immediate event on December 25, 1845 of priest Vertanes' firm refusal to listen to the Patriarch's counsel to be obedient to the "Holy Church," and his denial of the holy mysteries of the church. He refused to believe that the bread and wine in the Communion are transformed into the body and blood of Christ, that confession of sins and the veneration of the cross are necessary, that Mary was virgin until her ascension to the throne. Priest Vertanes, according to historian Berberian, Chairman of the Council of the Patriarchate and the recorder of the event, is supposed to have stated "impiously" about Mary: "Why give so much respect and honor to an unchaste woman?" Thereupon, the "representative" of the Patriarch, Vartabed Tateos, grew madly angry and wanted to smash the head of the "impious" priest saying, "Let such unlawful and impious persons die and perish from upon the face of the earth and let my blood flow for the sake of the Mother of God."[53] The situation was restored by the Patriarch, who, after ordering Vertanes out of the room, held Vartabed Tateos back from his intent. The following day, the public having heard of the happenings, many church leaders and honorable men

49. Armenian for "No."
50. For the text of the excommunication decree see Appendix.
51. Berberian, Kevork-Mesrob, Hamlin and Eutudjian give the date of the decree to be January 13, according to the Old School Calendar.
52. R. Anderson, *History of the Missions of the American Board of Commissioners for Foreign Missions to the Oriental Churches* (Boston: Congregational Publishing Society, 1872), p. 394; Dwight, *op. cit.*, p. 215; Eutudjian, *op. cit.*, p. 151; Prime, *op. cit.*, p. 307; Hamlin, *op. cit.*, p. 132; Kevork-Mesrob, *op. cit.*, p. 516.
53. Berberian, *op. cit.*, p. 298.

came to the Patriarch to protest against all such "unrighteous" men who were *preaching false teachings in the market places and coffee shops and calling the Armenians idolaters.* They said the agitation may not be withstood by men who are ignorant but zealous of their faith, such as water-bearers and sailors. These intemperate and ignorant men may cause death by killing one of the converts, as a result of which the ambassadors of England and America may accuse the Armenians of being barbarous murderers of the Protestants. So, they asked the Patriarch: "It is up to you, holy Father, to anticipate the tragic evil and find a solution because the Armenians are not on speaking terms with the sectarians, neither do they enter their homes or stores to do business with them." [54] Berberian further states that the Patriarch then invited the past-Patriarch Garabed, Archbishop Hovhannes of the Convent of Jerusalem, and the elderly Vartabed Hovhannes. He told them of the incident and they decided unanimously to issue a "decree of excommunication" [55] on January 12, 1846, [56] to be read the following Sunday in all the churches of Constantinople and a copy was sent to the interior of Turkey. [57]

This first bull of excommunication [58] stated that the leaders of the Church must "keep that which is committed to their trust" avoiding profane and vain babblings and oppositions of science falsely so called [59] and spoke of how in "these latter days" some have departed from the holy faith due to new-fangled oppositions and errors. Then, it named one person in the nation, "a contemptible wretch, the unworthy priest Vertanes of Nicomedia. . . ." who "like a vagabond going about . . . babbles out errors, unworthy of his sacred office and dignity, and becomes an occasion of stumbling to others."

After speaking of the priest's obstinacy in not hearkening to the good counsel of his lordship, and of the danger to the spiritual welfare of his flock involved in the free access to the community of such a "traitor and murderer of Christ," the Patriarch concluded:

> Wherefore we expel him and forbid him as a Devil, and a child of the Devil, to enter the company of our believers. We cut him off from the priesthood as an amputated member of the spiritual body of Christ, and as

54. Berberian, *op. cit.,* p. 229.
55. A term used by contemporary Berberian, but Yeghiayan, in his anxiety to prove his point that there was no excommunication says, *"But no such thing existed in reality . . . it was a paper of defrocking."* Chapter 10, p. 15. (In published work, p. 245.)
56. According to Old School Calendar, new being January 25, 1846.
57. Berberian, *op. cit.,* pp. 297-303; Yeghiayan, *op. cit.,* Chapter 10, pp. 13-14. (In published work, p. 243-244.)
58. Berberian, *op. cit.,* pp. 299-303, for original in Armenian; *Missionary Herald,* June, 1846, pp. 196 f., and Dwight, *op. cit.,* pp. 323 f. for the English translation. In this work see Appendix: "First Anathema of the Priest Vertanes."
59. I Tim. 6:20.

a branch cut off from the vine, which is good for nothing but to be cast into the fire. By this admonitory bull, I therefore command and warn my beloved in every city, far and near, not to look upon his face, regarding it as the face of Belial; not to receive him into your holy dwelling, for he is a house-destroying and ravening wolf; not to receive his salutation, but as a soul-destroying and deadly poison; and to beware, with all your households, of the seducing and impious followers, of the false doctrine of MODERN SECTARIES. . . .[60]

If peace was to be sought, the decree was doing nothing to bring it about. It was an "angering" solution.[61]

After the excision of Vertanes, the evangelicals were called up one by one by the Patriarch and required to sign the "Paper of Recantation," declaring that they were "deceived by the wicked enticements of Satan" and affirming that "the faith of the holy church is spotless, her sacraments divine, her rites of apostolic origin, her ritual pious."[62] Having so affirmed, they were to renounce all further communication with the new sectaries. But, during the first week following the excision of Vertanes, none of the evangelicals affixed his signature to this document. The following Sunday, therefore, the Patriarch issued a more emphatic anathema, and explained that "the decree of Anathema was read for the information of the pious, but some of the people understood it as referring only to the cursed nonentity Vertanes, falsely called priest, and not also to the others. Wherefore we considered it necessary today to repeat it, and to inform you, that not only the accursed one (Vertanes), but also all that are of his sentiments, deceivers and blasphemers against the Church, and followers of *the corrupt new sect*, are accursed and excommunicated and anathemized, by God, and by all his saints, and by us." Having said this he continued to instruct:

> Wherefore, whoever has a son, that is such an one, or a brother, or a partner, and *gives him bread,* or *assists him in making money,* or *has intercourse with him as a friend,* or *does business with him*—let such persons know that they are nourishing a venomous serpent in their houses, which will one day injure them with its deadly poison, and they will lose

---

60. Dwight, *op. cit.,* pp. 323 f.; Berberian, *op. cit.,* pp. 299 f.
61. We are in accord with Yeghiayan that this was not an "excommunication decree" against the entire Evangelical movement but simply a "paper depriving a priest from grace," despite the presence of the words to be careful of "the seducing and impious followers of the false doctrine of Modern Sectaries . . ." But, we cannot grant that the decree would pacify excited passions. Unfortunately, Yeghiayan ignores to refer to a second decree of excommunication against all who were of Vertanes' sentiments—"followers," as the instrument reads . . . "of the corrupt new sect, who are accursed, excommunicated, and anathemized." See Yeghiayan, *op. cit.,* Ch. 10, p. 15 (In published work, p. 245); Anderson, *op. cit.,* Vol. I p. 394; Strong, *op. cit.,* p. 105; Prime, *op. cit.,* p. 308; Dwight, *op. cit.,* p. 219; Appendix in this work entitled: "Second Anathema of the Armenian Patriarch."
62. Dwight, *op. cit.,* pp. 327 f.; Appendix: "The Paper of Recantation."

their souls. Such persons give bread to Judas. Such persons are enemies of the holy faith of Christianity, and destroyers of the holy orthodox Church of the Armenians, and a disgrace to the whole nation. Wherefore, *their houses and shops also are accursed;* and *whoever* goes to visit them, we shall learn and make them public to the holy Church by *terrible* anathemas.[63]

Surely, the decrees of excommunication, placed side by side with the "Paper of Recantation" and the "New Creed" as well as the "Reply" to the letter of "The Persecuted Christians," are ample evidence that all the other reasons given for the commencing of coercions upon the Evangelicals were mere occasions for action there being more basic questions at issue. Those basic issues would not and could not let the Church leadership stand by idly or be apathetic. The Church leaders had to take a stand on important questions like the following, for which the traditions of the Armenian Church had formulated answers:

"Is any Christian group or individual entitled to the formulation of a Creed, the interpretation of Scripture, and the guaranteeing of salvation outside the traditions of the Church and its sacraments? Are Christians who are void of the Apostolic Succession entitled to pass decisions that the Bible must not be supplemented by the traditions of the Universal Church? Shall Christians who do not have Apostolic Succession through the laying on of hands by episcopal bishops have authority in the Church or in Church matters? Can the Church err even if its religious officers lived unworthy lives?" The ringing, dogmatic answers to these questions were, "No."[64]

It was an unyielding and inflexible position, and one wishes that more moderating influences had been at work. But it does not mean that it was

---

63. Dwight, *Ibid.,* pp. 326 f.; Appendix: "Second Anathema of the Armenian Patriarch."

Berberian, without saying whether it was on the occasion of the reading of the first or second decree, writes that "unfaithful Voskan, Boghos and Hovsep Kamaghielian brothers, cantor Apissoghom, Mirikelam Garabed, Stepan Kerestedjian," followers of Vertanes, were also anathemized. We can safely assume that it was during the reading of the second anathema, since the second decree was given for clarification that more than Vertanes was meant. Therefore, Yeghiayan shortchanges the Evangelicals when he says that in the four printed pages of the decree nowhere is there . . ." a sentence that is concerning general protestantism, or concerning the missionaries, but that it is only and only about the priest mentioned." Neither is he justified in criticising Y. Kassouny's phrase, "The decree is written in such accusatory and condemnatory words that we refrain from quoting to be careful not to soil our pages." Yeghiayan assumes that Kassouny is refraining from quoting for fear he would expose himself, since the decree is harmless. Kevork-Mesrob concedes there was a second decree which excommunicated all those who had accepted protestantism. See Berberian, *op. cit.,* p. 303; Yeghiayan, *op. cit.,* Chapter 10, p. 16-17 (In published work, pp. 245-247); Kassouny, *Loossashavigh,* p. 37; Kevork-Mesrob, *op. cit.,* p. 517, quoted from Hrant Asadour's *The Armenians of Constantinople and Their Patriarchs* (Extensive Almanac of the National Sanatorium, 1901), pp. 208 f.

64. Patriarchate, "Proclamation One," *op. cit.,* pp. 1-47; "Paper of Recantation" in Appendix in this work.

a selfish stand. This sympathy must be granted, because for a nation which had had a stormy political history, the permanence envisioned in an authoritarian Church was a necessarily attractive concept. If the Church were to lose that unity guaranteed by its authoritative policy, more voices would have been added to the already babel of noises with which the nation was plagued. The nation had experienced political disunity with disastrous results; it assumed, therefore, spiritual disunity would bring about similar results. Actually, the new doctrines were at serious variance with the doctrines of the Apostolic Church and what was being asked was a surrender to a Protestant way of Church life. This was not granted, then, and neither is it granted now, after more than twelve decades.

Between the first decree of excommunication on January 25, 1846, and the permanent decree of excommunication issued on June 21, 1846, the battle raged over doctrinal issues—as has been pointed out. On June 21, 1846, a decree of a more permanent nature was issued. This third decree[65] was a perpetual one not alone because the Patriarch issued it against all who remained firm to evangelical principles, but also because it was issued on the great feast day of Holy Echmiadzin with the instruction that it be publicly read, in all the Armenian churches throughout the empire, *at each annual return of the great feast day.*[66] What occurred in western Europe at the time of the Lutheran Reformation was now repeated on a smaller scale in the Armenian Church. The reformers, originally a party within the church, excluded from the Church's fellowship and ordinances, found themselves under the necessity of forming a rival organization outside the Church.[67]

F. The Founding of the First Evangelical Church of Armenia

On the first day of July, 1846[68] the "Evangelicals" entered into solemn covenant to form "The First Evangelical Armenian Church of Constantinople."[69] The service establishing the new church was held in the home of missionary Dwight and the platform or constitution, according to Goodell, was prepared with the advice of the missionaries. Forty mem-

65. Anderson, *op. cit.*, pp. 416-417.
66. *Ibid.;* Dwight, *op. cit.*, p. 263; Prime, *op. cit.*, p. 316; Kevork-Mesrob, *op. cit.*, p. 518; Arpee, *Armenian Awakening,* p. 132.
67. Arpee, *Armenian Awakening,* p. 132.
68. Eutudjian, *op. cit.*, p. 166.
69. A.B.C.F.M., *Annual Report,* pp. 52 f.; Prime, *op cit.*, pp. 316-322.

bers,[70] thirty-seven male and three female, became the founding members and chose Apissoghom Khachadoorian (Eutudjian) the same day to become the first pastor[71] of THE FIRST EVANGELICAL AR-MENIAN CHURCH OF CONSTANTINOPLE. He was ordained on July 7, 1846, with the American missionaries and the Reverend Mr. Allan of the Free Church of Scotland taking part in the service.[72]

Numerous reasons are given to justify this final separation. The Armenian "Evangelicals" claim, first of all, that their "special purpose of enlightening and reforming the Church" from "those human traditions and ceremonies which are opposed to the rules of the Bible" was not accepted.[73] Second, a specifically formulated Creed, containing the very same ecclesiastical traditions unacceptable to the dissidents, was presented for acceptance and subscription.[74] The Evangelicals interpreted this to mean that the Armenian Church was neither ready nor willing to make any compromises. Third, they claimed they were persecuted[75] and cited a long list of grievances: a) economic boycott; b) social

70. Membership by the end of 1846 had grown to 140 and the number of churches to 4. After that the Evangelical Movement grew substantially, as the following chart will show:

	1846	1872	1914
Churches	4	76	137
Communicant Members	140	4,632	13,891
Protestant Community	1,000	19,471	50,900
Ministers and Evangelists	1	106	179
Teachers	1	500	850
Primary Schools	0	222	369
Primary School Students	0	5,080	19,400
Sunday School Pupils	0	8,790	22,700
Annual Contributions for Church Work	0	$12,139	$192,000

By 1895, there were eight high schools for girls, two colleges and one Collegiate Institute. There were eight colleges, five seminaries, and forty-four high schools with boarding departments, spread over Cilician Armenia, whose population was variously estimated from 1-1/2 to 2-1/2 million.

71. Dwight, *op. cit.*, p. 265; Strong, *op. cit.*, p. 105; Eutudjian, *op. cit.*, pp. 167 f.

72. Prime, *op. cit.*, p. 318.

73. Appendix, DECLARATION OF REASONS FOR ORGANIZING PROTESTANT CHURCHES.

74. *Ibid.*

75. Southgate, Berberian, and Yeghiayan do not agree that there was any persecution despite Archbishop Ormanian's acceptance of its existence. Bishop Horatio Southgate, missionary of the Episcopal Church of America to Constantinople and who had begun an ecclesiastical-theological controversy and challenged the methods and motives of the missionaries of the American Board, held that the Armenian Patriarch was within his rights in his acts not having gone beyond the proper limits of his authority. He considered that all statements against the Patriarch were "without exception, gross fabrications," and hoped that all the seceders would "return to the quiet performance of religious duty, in the Church in which they were baptized." (See, *Christian Witness and Church Advocate,* May 15, 1846, as quoted in Dwight, *op. cit.*, p. 243; *ibid.*, June 26, 1846; "Letters to the Missionaries of the American Board in Constantinople," (Dec. 4, 1843); "Vindication of the Rev. Horatio Southgate," (Jan. 9, 1844). Berberian, on whose writing Yeghiayan depends and with whom he agrees, says that the Patriarch was doing his God-given duty and that if the Patriarch had

ostracism; c) absence of restraint on populace from engaging in fierce social pressures; d) banishment of priests and teachers; e) stoning, hanging up by the thumbs, spitting and smiting in the face, torturing with the bastinado, and imprisonment without open charge or trial; f) intimidation to force the signing of the contents of decrees; g) mob invasion of the houses of dissidents and the destruction of property; and h) the encouragement by the church authorities to disinherit[76] or expel members of the families if they followed the "evangelical way."[77] Fourth, despite their claim to be faithful and orthodox Christians who adhered to the Nicene Creed[78] the Armenian Church anathemized and excommunicated them. Thus excommunicated for their divergence of opinion with the existing condition of the Church, they were deprived of fellowship with their Armenian brethren as well as the ordinances of the Church. The prohibitions left the Evangelicals no one who could administer them the sacraments of the Armenian Church, except on acceptance of the decrees and documents of penitence. The fifth reason for the necessity of separation was the concern of the Evangelicals for the religious training of their children. Since they were convinced that the Christian faith as interpreted by the American missionaries was correct

not taken the precautions which he did, he would have acted irresponsibly. Addressing himself to Armenian Evangelical authors Yeghiayan says that the thesis that there was persecution "has become a fable" and is simply "self-justification." (See, Yeghiayan, *op. cit.,* Chapters 8, pp. 3 and 11, p. 26—In published work, pp. 168-169 and 259 respectively).

76. Missionary Dwight provides a letter signed and sealed by the Patriarch in order to demonstrate the coercion that went so far as to demand disinheritance. We provide this letter as follows:

My beloved priest,—This Khachadoor, a penitent, has said 'I have sinned,' and promised to confess to you, and to commune in the bosom of our Church. But his three sons are impenitent and hardened in inquiry. If they come to the house of their father, he is not to receive them, and he is not to retain them as his heirs; but let them be stripped of their inheritance, if they do not turn from their wickedness. Farewell.

(Dated January 18 (O.S.), 1846
At the Patriarchate of the
Armenians
Constantinople
(Sealed)   Matteos
Patriarch

(See Dwight, *op. cit.,* p. 219).

77. For these and similar acts of persecution see the following sources: *A.B.C.F.M., Annual Report,* 1846, pp. 98-99 (Footnote); Anderson, *op. cit.,* pp. 212-214; Appendix, "Declaration of Reasons for Organizing Protestant Churches;" Dwight, *op. cit.,* pp. 217-218; Eutudjian, *op. cit.,* pp. 136-148; 160-162; 169-172; Hamlin, *op. cit.,* p. 133; Y. Kassouny, *Loossashavigh,* pp. 25, 32, 39-40; Prime, *op. cit.,* p. 309; Strong, *op. cit.,* p. 104; Ohan Gaydzakian, *Illustrated Armenia and the Armenians* (Boston, 1898), for a personal testimony that records: "I myself was beaten and imprisoned three times. I had to keep my Testament in my pocket for three months, could not read it openly, but had to look for secluded places to read the words of life."

78. An interesting and productive research could be made into the possibility of the Nicene Creed becoming the basis for Protestant-Apostolic Union.

because of its recognition of the Bible as the only rule of faith and conduct, they desired that their children be raised accordingly. *The Evangelicals did not think that the American missionaries were bringing a new faith and theology to them. They only concurred with them that the Bible should become the sole authority in Christian faith and conduct.*

The Evangelicals insist that they tried not to separate. They refer, beside the letter entitled "Persecuted Christians," to three other efforts to avert the separation: 1) their appeal to the Armenian magnates who did not dignify them with a reply; [79] 2) their letter to Rashid Pasha, Turkish Minister of Foreign Affairs, in the middle of February, 1846, defining their grievances against the Patriarch. The influence of Armenians in office at the Porte prevented a favorable solution to the problem; [80] 3) their letter to the Ambassadors of England, Prussia, and America asking for their influence to procure release from suffering and a guarantee of their civil rights. As a result of this the Evangelicals were permitted to become sureties for one another—a method of getting over the alleged legal difficulties.

The Armenian Church authorities, apparently, did not attempt to reduce the polarization, for, having stopped the open civil persecution due to the last step listed above, the New Creed was still presented for signature and the anathemas still resounded from the pulpits, according to Goodell, causing great agitation among the Apostolic faithful against the Evangelicals. Public resentment continued to increase, the Apostolic side felt justified to be firm, and the position of the Evangelicals was stiffened. The cup was full for both sides. The answer, the missionaries and the Armenian Evangelicals became convinced, was to separate.

Religious awakening is a powerful force. But when an already Christian people, as the Armenians were, are reawakened an additional emotional and psychological dimension is introduced and the power is even greater. Goodell and other American Board missionaries may repeat their refrain that they did not stand for a narrow policy and did not wish to separate any one. Yet, deep down in their heart they knew that to "enlighten, and improve, and elevate" was laying the seed for separation. The enlightened could not have stayed indifferent to the inadequacies in their Church and they did not. To quote A.A. Bedikian:

79. Prime, *op. cit.*, p. 310; Dwight, *op. cit.*, p. 234.
80. Dwight, *op. cit.*, p. 235; Prime, *op. cit.*, p. 310.

It is impossible to be nurtured by the Gospel in its purity and at the same time view with indifference theories, doctrines, traditions, mores, customs and social practices in and outside the church which did not, in a strict sense, harmonize with the Gospel.[81]

That is why neither the attempts to win the dissidents by persuasion, debates, lectures and discourses nor the intimidations by persecution and excommunication succeeded in avoiding a final separation. Accommodation and compromise might have helped "defuse" the heat but the Armenian Church and lay leadership were not willing to entertain that kind of solution.

81. A.A. Bedikian, *op. cit.*, p. 10.

PART THREE

OTHER FACTORS AIDING
THE SEPARATION

CHAPTER VIII

THE RADICAL PROTEST
OF THE REFORMED

In part one of this research we have seen that the combined effect of the traditions, purposes, methods and activities of the missionaries was to create a serious conflict between them and the Armenian Church and to cause a polarization full of possibilities for a schism. In part two, it was observed that reform trends in the Armenian Church had always been negated and that in respect to the American mission the Armenian Church soon developed strong opposition which took the extreme form of excommunication of those in favor of the theology and the church discipline of the American missionaries. The combined effect of the polarization was the decision on the part of the "evangelically-minded" to found a separate Church with a covenant for membership.

In this portion, namely part three, it will be demonstrated that two other factors aided the separation:

1) the radical protest of the "reformed" or "awakened;" [1]

2) reform trends in Turkey and the influence of western European representatives in Constantinople.

A. Persecution and the Awakened

Opinion among the Armenian leadership was divided over the application of strict measures against the awakened. Patriarchs Hagopos and Matteos believed they could arrest the movement by strictness, as opposed to Patriarch Stepanos who held that strictness causes reaction and persecution leads to the dissemination of the very ideas that are unacceptable. Patriarch Stepanos proved to be correct, for persecution stiffened the resistance of the awakened and flagged the zeal of men who had come under the power of the Gospel. Afflictions and persecutions deepened their convictions.

---

1. "reformed" and "awakened" are used in the sense of conversion from an "unregenerate" to a "regenerate" condition of Christian existence reminiscent of the conversions during the Great Awakening in the American colonies of the eighteenth century.

For instance, one convert who had been a colporteur had lost his vineyards and mulberry orchards and had endured violence. He said of his sufferings for Christ's sake:

> The truth in my heart was like a stake slightly driven into soft ground, easily swayed, and in danger of falling before the wind; but by the sledge-hammer of persecution God drove it in till it became immovable. [2]

Another convert indicated his steadfastness in the face of hardship thus:

> My daily prayer to God is, that even if there should not be left a single person except myself to witness for the truth, He would still give me faith to stand firm for the doctrine of salvation by grace in Christ alone. I know that all the resistance we now make to error, we are making for coming generations. We may never reap the fruits ourselves, but our exercise of firmness and faith now, will enable thousands, and perhaps millions, in after days to enjoy the rights of conscience in pure and holy worship. [3]

Persecution led others to be willing to share the fate of the persecuted. The story is told of five evangelicals who were taken to the convent of Armash in Caesaria and there imprisoned. Many persons walked to the convent, on learning their imprisonment was for considering the Bible to be the only authoritative religious guide, and said to the abbot: "We are of the same sentiments with these men, and we wish to share in their trials." [4] One effect of the persecutions therefore was to make the converts zealous and to deepen their convictions.

A second effect was to make the converted vocal against the biblical ignorance of the priests, thus turning them into self-proclaimed "evangelists" or "missionaries." The challenge against biblical ignorance is appropriately illustrated with the following incident. A priest, on a mission to a family to caution them of the dangers of following the American teachings, was questioned by the son of the couple who had embraced "evangelical" principles. The priest, according to Dwight, consistently changed the subject, leading the mother to rebuke the priest who was normally highly respected:

> What! are you already tired of talking about the Bible, that you have so soon laid it aside? Are you not a priest, and can you find anything more important to talk about? Now, I wish to ask you one question. Do you suppose that when our Savior first instituted the Lord's Supper, he wore those splendid robes, and that mitre set with diamonds, and carried such a golden staff as our bishops do at mass? [5]

2. Strong, *op. cit.*, p. 219.
3. Dwight, *op. cit.*, pp. 232 f.
4. *Ibid.*, p. 207; Tracey, *op. cit.*, p. 387.
5. Dwight, *op. cit.*, p. 72.

Challenging the inadequate ministry rendered by the clergy of the Armenian Church in such manners, the awakened or regenerated were goaded by the restrictions to exert greater effort to minister God's word to their countrymen. At their own expense, several of the regenerated sent one of their number "on a missionary tour among the Armenians in the interior of Asia Minor," the commissioned person being priest Vertanes. [6] On Sundays, the converted turned into preachers to acquaint their friends and acquaintances with the Gospel. [7]

A third effect was to make them zealous in the application of the truths learned to their lives. They developed an applied piety and used it as a challenge to priests, who, they assumed, were neglectful in their conduct. A man in Broosa, a picture-maker for the Church by trade, soon resolved to relinquish this employment because it depended upon "idolatry" for its support.[8] Once, five priests went to the house of Surpuhie Nergararian [9] and told her that she must turn over the Protestant Bible because the Scriptures must be interpreted by the Church and not individually by a person. She was indignant and said:

> . . . since my husband has read this book, he has become a *temperate* man, *kind* and *indulgent* to his family, but to whom you never before came to advise as to his conduct. But now, since he has been reformed by the reading of this book, *five* of you *long bearded* priests, who heretofore never inquired into our spiritual condition, now come to advise and dictate to us what we shall do; are you therefore not ashamed to ask for it? [10]

The same taunt was cast in the face of the Bishop of Nicomedia when he asked Haroutune Zeparar if he were not dishonoring his father-in-law by following the evangelical heresy. Said he, "*I greatly dishonored* him when I sought pleasure in the public wine houses. I was a lost sheep, but none came to seek me, for the shepherd of the flock was an hireling. But I have found the true shepherd the Bishop of my soul who gave his life for me." [11]

The fourth effect of the persecution was to make the converts ready to suffer for their beliefs. Their earnestness led them to suffer privations, persecutions, and insults patiently and nobly. For instance when Der Haroutune of Nicomedia refused to sign the paper of recantation he was thrown out of the church, where he had gone to conduct services, with kicks and blows. The most humiliating insult that could have been heaped upon a priest was his lot. His hair and his sacerdotal beard were sheared,

---

6. Prime, *op. cit.*, pp. 280 f; Dwight, *op. cit.*, pp. 141 f.
7. Prime, *Ibid.*, p. 265.
8. Dwight, *op. cit.*, p. 150.
9. The mother of author Garabed Nergararian.
10. Garabed Nergararian, *A Brief History of the Beginning of the Mission Work in Nicomedia* (Waynesboro, Pennsylvania: Gazette Steam Printing House, 1885), pp. 15 f.
11. *Ibid.*, p. 19.

and as he was cast out of the church, the mob called out "accursed." He was also imprisoned. Haroutune, in consequence, wrote: "I entered the prison with a joyful heart, committing myself to God, and giving glory to him that he had enabled me to pass through fire and sword. . . . And now I am dead to my former character and position. I obtained a new life in Christ."[12] Not priests alone, but ordinary businessmen withstood troubles joyfully. A shopkeeper, who on receiving the gospel had lost all his goods, was driven from his father's house, attacked in the streets, knocked down, and beaten. On the following day, he was given a shocking fright in his store, as a result of which he commenced hemorrhaging. While dying, he exclaimed, "Glory to God that He has condescended to call me into the light of His glorious Gospel! Blessed be His name that I have been made acquainted with my former errors in time, and that the true Gospel has been made known to me!"[13] Others, driven from their homes and having become dependent upon the compassion of foreign sympathy fasted, prayed, and sang hymns of praise with unshaken confidence and bore their troubles quietly and nobly.[14] Goodell immortalized the steadfastness of the converted under tribulation in the following passage:

> Their songs of praise from the whole congregation went up like the sound of many waters, and reminded me of the singing of the ancient Bohemian brethren amidst the raging fires of persecution. And, indeed, to see them stand . . . with such firmness on the Rock of eternal ages . . . to see them take joyfully the spoiling of their goods . . . was a spectacle for angels and for men.[15]

These responses to the hardships caused by their religious convictions can hardly be explained away by the charge that they were "purchased by money." They appear to be genuinely "regenerated" persons,[16] whose convictions were costing them pain, suffering and loss. A special dynamism is evidenced in their conduct, injected into them by their new convictions, but heightened by the intimidations and persecutions of the Armenian Church authorities.

All in all, the persecution served as an advantage to the Armenian Evangelicals: it stimulated choice brave young men, whose influence became important later on, to join the American Seminary;[17] it excited

---

12. Dwight, *op. cit.*, p. 250; Arpee, *Awakening*, p. 34; Anderson, *op. cit.*, Vol. I, pp. 404 f.
13. Prime, *op. cit.*, pp. 323 f.
14. *Ibid.*, p. 311; Hamlin, *op. cit.*, p. 133.
15. Prime, *op. cit.*, p. 311.
16. This researcher is not arguing for or against the correctness or incorrectness of the theology and beliefs of these "regenerated" individuals—a subject which could well be a source for another dissertation.
17. Hamlin, *op. cit.*, p. 134.

extensive attention among the villagers who wanted to know what "Protestantism"[18] was; it caused the spread of evangelicalism; it turned the convictions of the persecuted more pronounced;[19] it gave the American missionaries "justification" to plan and act more independently from the Armenian Church.[20]

B. The Nature of the Protest of the Regenerated

The nature of the protest of the awakened was as radical as their reaction to persecution was strong and vocal. They found the theology and ceremonies of the Armenian Church unacceptable on the ground that instead of being based on the teachings of the Bible, they were founded on "human inventions"—not on the inspiration of the Scriptures. When a convert was asked why he had forsaken the Armenian Church, his reply was: "It is the Gospel that I have received in the place of human inventions."[21] The reformed or regenerated Armenians developed a great reverence and love for the Bible, with a parallel disenchantment with the forms and rites of the Church which they felt were introduced by human beings. Their protest was that the old venerable Church had lost its original New Testament "simplicity" and "purity" and that it should return to that "pure" evangelical form.[22]

Undoubtedly, there was a close identity between this radical protest and the thinking of the missionaries who taught that all Christian practice should flow from the teaching of the Scriptures, specially the "Evangelion." The literature they offered to the Armenians propagated what they called the "evangelical"[23] truths. Reference has already been made to Legh Richmond's [24] "The Dairyman's Daughter," and "The Young Cottager." Couched underneath the stories, which relate the manner and effect of the regeneration of two young girls, is this "evangelical" theology:

1) that there is no pardon to the dead;
2) that careless repetition of the catechism is not religion;

18. Tracey, *op. cit.,* p. 16.
19. Eutudjian, *op. cit.,* p. 102.
20. Kassouny, *Loossashavigh,* p. 26; Hamlin, *op. cit.,* p. 61; Tracey, *op. cit.,* p. 389.
21. Prime, *op. cit.,* p. 323.
22. Kassouny, *Loossashavigh,* p. 51; Eutudjian, *op. cit.,* p. 55.
23. Meaning that truths arose out of the "Evangelion" which in turn was understood to mean the entire New Testament.
24. Legh Richmond, "The Dairyman's Daughter," (New York: American Tract Society, 1823-1827, as printed in *Annals of the Poor,* Philadelphia: Pres. Board of Publications); "The Young Cottager," (New York: American Tract Society).

3) that one becomes a child of God by God's grace, not by works;

4) that the Scriptures are needful for inspiration;

5) that the Lord's Supper is open only to one who is ready to examine himself, purpose in his heart to lead a new life, have a lively faith in God's mercy through Christ, have a thankful remembrance of his death, and live in charity with all men.

The radicalism of the regenerate arose out of the deep spirituality they came to develop. This depth of spirituality is attested to by statements that appeared in the Annual Report of the American Board.[25] The following are the testimonies about the awakened Armenians:

1) they were anxious to hear the preaching of the missionaries;

2) they excitedly sought answers to important and fundamental questions;

3) they showed increasing conviction of the enormous evil of sin and a disposition to search deeply their own hearts and to compare their secret thoughts and motives with the standard of God's word;

4) they understood "born again" to mean "an entire moral change."

5) they developed a genuine interest in the condition of others and decided to labor for the salvation of their countrymen with great enthusiasm.

Wach has pointed out that, in religious conflicts, during the period between individual protest and complete separation those involved advocate "a characteristic attitude, forms of devotion, or concepts which frequently aim at the eventual conversion of the entire community. They consider themselves as the 'leaven of the Gospel.' "[26]

In the case of the Armenian Evangelicals, Wach's statement held true. The Evangelicals did come to have attitudes and forms of worship which aimed at the eventual conversion of the entire Armenian nation. They desired to realize on earth the perfect church order, cleansed of corruption and purified of all unregeneracy. They wanted to bring the entire Armenian nation into "their" kind of regenerate condition. The slogan was to make the nation come alive again to true Christianity and the excitement in their heart was best expressed in Isaiah's words:

> Awake, awake; put on thy strength O Zion; put on thy beautiful garments, O Jerusalem, the holy city: for thenceforth there shall no more come into thee the uncircumcised.[27]

It is in this light that we must interpret the role of Der Sahakian, Minassian, and Sarkis Varjabed who banded together in the love of Christ with a "perfect readiness to go wherever duty shall call for the spiritual

25. *A.B.C.F.M., Annual Report,* 1845, pp. 92-95.
26. Wach, *op. cit.,* p. 174.
27. Isaiah 52:1.

benefit of the Armenian nation,"[28] and vowed "to labor for our nation while we live."[29]

In this intense desire for a purified and perfect church order we see a point of contact with the ideal of the American missionaries whose Puritan background prompted them to dream of that same perfect church order. Perry Miller, in his *New England Mind*, formulates that ideal of the New England Puritans in these words:

> Flowing from piety, from the tremendous thrust of the Reformation and the living force of Theology, came a desire to realize on earth the perfect church order.[30]

Goodell and Dwight and the other missionaries were motivated by the same ideal which they had also managed to transmit to the Armenians in Constantinople who were regenerated.

The Armenian Church as a whole, with a history of objection to reform, saw tragedy in this ideal; Armenians interested in vital spirituality welcomed the ideal and purpose. It was unfortunate, perhaps, that the religious and theological histories of the two traditions were to follow the inevitable sociological tendencies and bring about the separation.

C. Secession the Sociological Consequence of Radical Confrontation

Wach, analysing periodic protests against main trends world religions experience, argues as follows:

> All world religions face periodic protests against the main trend of their development. These occur in all three fields of religious expression—in theology, in cult, in organization. The protests are directed, on the one hand against the excessive expansion of the ecclesiastical body with its accompanying compromises and modifications and on the other, against individual shortcomings and defaults of a complacent body which looks with lack-luster eyes upon the possibilities of further growth and development.[31]

Wach shows further how *"ecclesiola in ecclesia"* develop in protest movements, which, "for lack of a better term" he calls *collegia pietatis*. He explains these to be "loosely organized groups, limited in numbers and

28. Missionary Herald, Vol. XXXII, February, 1836, p. 42.
29. *Ibid.*, December, p. 453.
30. Perry Miller, *New England Mind: From Colony to Province* (Cambridge: Harvard University Press, 1953), p. 440.
31. Wach, *op. cit.*, p. 156.

united in common enthusiasm, peculiar convictions, intense devotion, and rigid discipline" which strive to achieve higher spiritual and moral perfection than can be realized under prevailing conditions.[32] "In these *collegia,*" he writes, "the attempt is often to revert to the experience of the beginning in order to recapture the 'inspiration' of the founder and his circle. . . . The driving power of the movement may be the desire for more intense individual experience or for a maximum of common standardized religious practices."[33]

The regenerated Armenians turned their criticism, paralleling Wach's analysis, to the suggested three areas: 1) the doctrinal tenets, 2) the ritual or elements in the cult, and 3) the organization of the Armenian Church. The awakened grouped themselves into a Society of the Pious and worked towards the achievement of higher spiritual and moral perfection on a personal and national level by returning to the Founder and His circle—to the Gospels of Jesus of Nazareth and the writings of the Apostles. Their Christian beliefs now livened up by a conversion experience into Christian convictions, they reflected upon some questions that had personal as well as national significance: could a regenerate person, who did not believe in the literal transformation of the "bread and the wine into the real body and blood of Christ" have communion in the Apostolic Church? Would such a person be willing to expose his children to the teaching he had come to reject? If salvation is not of, by or through the Armenian Church but through faith in Christ alone, could he possibly be spiritually benefited by attending the services of the Church? Would he be honest if he took his children to a Church that claimed it gave salvation, when it really could not? If these are fundamental truths, should he not be his brothers' keeper and alert them to the dangers to which their souls were exposed? As answers were formulated for these questions in their minds, the conviction grew that the alternative to worshiping hypocritically was to establish a church which could operate on "evangelical" lines. They needed freedom to worship according to their "regenerated" conscience, which the Armenian Church would not and could not grant; they wanted to work towards the salvation of souls within the bosom of the Church, which the Church could not permit; they wanted to participate in the Sacrament of Baptism and the Lord's Supper according to their own understanding, without the necessity of confessing to the priest for communion, but the Church would not allow it; they saw the necessity of providing a Bible-centered Christian education for their children, but knew that the Armenian Church could neither meet the necessary standards nor accept the innovation.

32. *Ibid.,* pp. 173 f.
33. *Ibid.,* pp. 176 f.

It is difficult to keep hungry men from looking for food and thirsty men from satisfying their thirst. From all evidence this researcher was able to muster, the converted felt spiritual hunger[34] and their emotions were pent-up and needed expanding. As Wach points out, "emotional starvation is one of the causes which produces sectarianism." [35]

The spiritual and emotional condition of the converted lead us to believe that Wallace's definition of a "religious revival" or "sect formation" as a revitalization movement is applicable to these persons. [36] In a revitalization movement there is a deliberate, organized conscious effort by members of a society to construct a more satisfying culture. The persons involved in the process of revitalization need, first of all, to perceive their culture, or some major areas of it, as a system. Second, they need to feel that this cultural system is unsatisfactory. Third, they need to decide to innovate a new cultural system. In the revitalization movement, change is not gradual, taking generations and centuries to come about. The required changes are shifted into a new Gestalt abruptly and, frequently within a few years, the new plan is put into effect by the participants in the movement. [37] In a rather unique way, this process of revitalization was at work among the Armenians in Constantinople. Armenians saw their Church and its religious and cultural expression as a system; they found this system unsatisfactory; they were stimulated to bring about a change of image. In their case the necessity of bringing about an innovation was quick, reaching a point of intensity within a space of fifteen years.

Wach has demonstrated validly that the social consequences of radical protest leads to secession generally. He sees the protest beginning as a reform movement from within, first, and then moving on until the reformer becomes a separatist. In the Armenian Church situation, the protest began as a reform movement from within, with no intention of schism; the radical attitude of the smaller group and the intransigent attitude of the mother institution grew too powerful to retain unity; the reformer became a separatist and the group an independent church.

34. A.B.C.F.M., *Annual Report,* 1845, pp. 92 f.
35. Wach, *op. cit.,* p. 161.
36. This researcher would like to grant that this identification may be challenged on the ground that the Armenian Evangelical schism was a contrived situation and was not a spontaneous expression. Wallace points out that the revitalization movement is usually conceived in a prophet's visions. In the case before us, the prophetic voice, it will be granted, came from outside the community—from the missionaries of the American Board. This does not, however, invalidate the process. The missionaries stimulated what was a need in existence among enlightened Armenians. They were not able to do the same, for instance, with the Moslem population because that group did not have the need to construct a more satisfying culture as much as the Armenians who were not first class citizens in the Ottoman Empire.
37. Wallace, *op. cit.,* p. 265.

Wach, writing in 1944 first, speaks as though he were describing the separation of the Armenian Evangelicals when he writes:

> The protest against conditions in the ecclesiastical body usually begins from within a reform movement, not necessarily with intentions of causing a schism, which, on the contrary, is, as we saw, more often than not anxiously avoided. The inner logic, vitality, or radicalism of the intransigent attitude of the mother community or its representatives, however, may prove more powerful than the good will of the dissenters, and a secession results. The reformer becomes a separatist, and the reform group an independent body or sect. [38]

The zeal, the Christian concern, and the emotional need of the reformed or regenerated had to have a positive and active expression. When the converted were unable to practice that expression within the Church organization because of the attitude of the mother community, the unsought secession came about.

It should be pointed out, however, that the Armenian Church authorities had the power to put an end to the separation or neutralize the work of the regenerated enthusiasts by the great authority the Patriarch had over his constituency—an authority granted him by Sultanic decree. The next chapter will demonstrate how that authority was by-passed and the separation was sustained.

38. Wach, *op. cit.*, p. 186.

CHAPTER IX

REFORM TRENDS IN TURKEY AND THE INFLUENCE OF WEST EUROPEAN REPRESENTATIVES IN CONSTANTINOPLE

Certain external factors became instrumental in bringing about the Evangelical separation. These were closely related to the decline of the Ottoman Empire and the subsequent plans of several Sultans to reform it. The presence of the European ambassadors mediated in bringing about a trend for religious freedom. The separatists, to obtain such religious freedom, received the assistance of ambassadors and through their mediation convinced the Porte to grant a *Millet* status. How such factors led to separation of the Armenian Protestants into a separate community is the task of this chapter.

A. The Decline of Turkey and the Turn to the West

The Turks, a nomadic people who adopted Islam as early as the eighth century, had expanded over the steppes of central Asia in the beginning of the seventh century and by the eleventh century had taken present-day Iraq, Syria, and Asia Minor. In 1071 the Seljuk Turks defeated the Byzantine forces in Armenia. After experiencing some reverses from the hordes of the Mongol Genghis Khan, they established, in the first quarter of the fourteenth century, the nucleus of an Ottoman Empire under Othman, the son of the Turkish chieftain Ertogrul. Under Mohammed III (1451-1481), on May 29, 1453, Constantinople was captured by the overthrow of the last stronghold of the Byzantine Empire. By the time of Sultan Suleiman the Magnificent (1520-1566), the empire had reached its zenith. During this peak, the Ottoman Empire ruled over a vast territory including Mesopotamia, Arabia, and Syria in Asia; Egypt, Tunis, Lybia, and Algeria in Africa; and the Balkan Peninsula and the Crimea in Europe.[1] Of course, Armenia was included in Mesopotamia.

After Suleiman's death the beginning of decay set in. The influence of the serai grew, grand viziers and ministers being appointed and dismissed under the influence of the harem. The sale of offices and heavy taxation contributed to political and economic instability. The power of the

---

1. Wayne S. Vucinich and Johnson E. Fairchild, "Turkey," *Collier's Encyclopedia*, 1957, Vol. XVIII, pp. 726-727.

Janissaries[2] increased and they controlled the government and the sultans. The Ruling and Moslem institutions began to break down, each usurping the other's functions.[3] The decline continued under Ibrahim (1640-1648), and a serious territorial recession was experienced by the Treaty of Karlowitz in 1699. The decline of the empire, principally because of poor organization and corruption, was further hastened by 1) the separatist tendencies of the oligarchs who ruled various provinces, 2) the growing strife between the various branches of administration, and 3) the inability of the government to ameliorate the social conditions caused by the disintegration of the feudal regime. Further weakening came, to add to the reasons given above, from 4) the system of "capitulations" giving foreign traders freedom from Turkish law and taxation, 5) the rising nationalistic ideas among the subject Christian peoples, and 6) the rebellions on the part of the Serbs (1804, 1815), and the Greeks (1821).[4] Stavrinos also stresses that the date to begin the transformation of the Ottoman Empire from an aggressive and feared force in European affairs to a helpless pawn of the Great Powers was 1699, following the Karlowitz Treaty.[5]

There was serious decline and sterility, also, in the arts and sciences. Stavrinos, quoting from William Eton's[6] *A Survey of the Turkish Empire,* writes:

> General knowledge is . . . little if at all cultivated. . . . The man of general science, a character so frequent and so useful in Christian Europe, is unknown. . . . The Natural consequence of these narrow views is that the professors of any art or science are themselves profoundly ignorant and that the greatest of absurdities are mixed with all their speculations "in Astronomy and Geography."[7]

These conditions led some to be concerned and look forward for improvements and changes. As early as the seventeenth century, Katib Chelibi, Turkish encyclopedist and historian, had warned his compatriots that Ottoman education had become static and sterile, but he was only a voice in the wilderness.[8] Towards the end of the eighteenth century, Abdul

2. Turkish, YENICHERI. Murad I (1359-1389) had devised a policy of incorporation and assimilation of the Christians into the Ottoman society through the famous *devchurme,* by which certain numbers of Christian boys were delivered at designated periods to the Ottoman authorities and converted to Islam. They were tutored as civil and military leaders, and filled the ranks of the standing infantry.
3. Vucinich and Fairchild, *op. cit.,* p. 727.
4. *Ibid.,* pp. 727-729.
5. Lefton Stavros Stavrinos. *The Ottoman Empire* (New York: Rinehart & Co., Inc., 1959), Second Printing, p. 32.
6. British Consul in Turkey and merchant.
7. Quoted in Stavrinos, *op. cit.,* p. 33.
8. *Ibid.,* p. 40.

Hamid I (1774-1789) attempted reforms in the military direction, chiefly because the Janissaries had degenerated into a lawless, undisciplined praetorian guard of the worst sort. With a view to reform the army "he imported some French officers in the hope that these might succeed in reorganizing the Janissaries and thus took the first step towards the Westernization of his country." [9]

Three consecutive Sultans attempted reforms systematically and aggressively. *SelimIII*(1789-1807) introduced the Nizam-i-jedid [10] which attempted to transform his empire along Western lines rather than go back to the good old days of Suleiman the Magnificient. [11] Unfortunately, reactionaries took instant dislike to the young Sovereign, and word spread that he was a Christian in disguise. [12] Opposition on the part of corrupt officials and the religious and military vested interests—the Ulema and the Janissaries—led to his dethronement in 1807. [13] *Mahmoud II* (1808-1839), Selim's successor, took up the fight for reform. He asserted his authority over the hitherto insubordinate Janissaries, Ulema, and other local potentates. [14] On June 10, 1826, his loyal troops mowed down one hundred thousand of the Janissaries. [15] Since his reforms had abolished the Court of Confiscations, provided the right for appeal, taken the Wakf property under State control, introduced European apparel, contemplated great reforms in favour of his Christian subjects and lost Greece and the Morea in 1821 and 1828 respectively, his death in 1839 caused joy to the officials and all "bigoted" Mohammedans. [16] Under *Abdul Mejid* (1839-1861), who ascended the throne in July, 1839 at the age of sixteen, "reform" became a program before which "even the mighty had to prostrate themselves."[17] His pro-Western grand vizier, Mustafa Reshid Pasha, who had been Turkey's ambassador to London, provided strong guidance. The years 1839-1861 became a period of frenzied reform. The young Sultan surrounded himself with men who were familiar with the orderly structure and operation of the West, and who were impressed by the public service of the West in contrast to that of Turkey which was service for privilege. These men were convinced that the salvation of Turkey lay in copying Britain's way of life. The result was that the Sultan

9. Sir Harry Luke, *The Making of Modern Turkey* (London: Macmillan and Co., Ltd., 1936), p. 31.
10. A term which may be translated to mean "the new organization" or "the new institutions."
11. Stavrinos, *op. cit.*, p. 40.
12. Lengyel, *op. cit.*, p. 272; Luke, *op. cit.*, p. 33.
13. Luke, *op. cit.*, p. 33.
14. Stavrinos, *op. cit.*, p. 40.
15. Lengyel, *op. cit.*, p. 274.
16. Prime, *op. cit.*, p. 24.
17. Lengyel, *op. cit.*, p. 281.

proclaimed the Tanzimat [18]—also known as the Hatt-i-Sheriff of Gulhane.[19]

Abdul Mejid's Hatt-i-Sheriff generated hope and great expectations among Armenians. It promised that "the cause of every accused person shall be publicly judged . . . and so long as a regular judgment shall not have been pronounced, no one can, secretly or publicly, put another to death by poison or in any other manner." It assured further, that "no one shall be allowed to attack the honor of any other person; each person shall possess his property of every kind, and shall dispose of it in all freedom without let or hindrance from any person whatsoever." It stipulated, in addition, that *"the Imperial concessions shall extend to all subjects, of whatever Religion or sect and that they will be granted perfect security in their lives, their honour, and their fortunes;* a rigorous Law shall be passed against the traffic of favouritism and of appointments."[20] Both in content and in the manner in which it was announced, the decree created a great stir. The young Sultan, for instance, ordered his grand vizier to read this formal "Bill of Rights" to an august assembly composed of the nobles of the empire, "not only Mussulmans, but the deputies of the Greeks, Armenians, and Jews, together with the ambassadors of the foreign powers."[21]

B. European Influence on Turkey

Whatever benefits these new trends might or might not have bestowed upon the Armenians,[22] the latter were very grateful for the European

---

18.   The plural of the Arabic Tanzim, meaning organization, ordering.
19.   Lengyel, *op. cit.,* p. 281. The Tanzimat, issued on Nov. 3, 1839, was followed by a second great landmark in the history of reform, namely the Hatt-i-Hymayun reform edict issued in February, 1857. It confirmed and consolidated the guarantees of security of personal property and of the preservation of the honour of all subjects of the Empire, without distinction of class or religion, promised in the Tanzimat. Together, these two decrees provide an important picture of the aspirations and objectives of the Turkish reformers and also reveal, by inference, the shortcomings and injustices that needed correction. (Luke, *op. cit.,* p. 50; Stavrinos, *op. cit.,* p. 40).
20.   Stavrinos, *op. cit.,* p. 41, quoted from Gulhane Decree from E. Hertslet, *The Map of Europe by Treaty* (4 vols; London, 1875-1891), II, 1002-1005. (Underlining is ours.)
21.   Prime, *op. cit.,* pp. 240 f.
22.   Historians differ, but most of them state that reforms were difficult to be made a real part of Turkey. (See Hamlin, *op. cit.,* pp. 47, 48, 55; Dwight, *op. cit.,* p. 106; Lengyel, *op. cit.,* pp. 28, 281; Luke, *op. cit.,* pp. 40, 52 which quotes from Ambassador Canning's statement; Stavrinos, *op. cit.,* p. 40 quoted from Great Britain, Accounts and Papers: State Papers, London, 1867, LXXV, 55-57, 77, 84-85. Grand Vizier, Fuad Pasha, however, in presenting the official Ottoman viewpoint argues that success had been attained in the implementation of the decrees. (See Stavrinos, *Ibid.,* pp. 45-46).

presence in Turkey. It was a consolation. It revealed to them a vision of existence wherein their dignity as human beings would be restored. They were encouraged in their hope that the West might open before Turkey the great possibilities the country had.

In a Turkey that was turning Westward, European influence was in evidence in military, political and economic areas. However, our interest is in the influence of Europeans on freedom of conscience in religious matters. For the development of this influence, we want to refer to the incident that enabled the European powers to wrest the principle of freedom of conscience in religion from the Ottoman Sultan.

The incident referred to is the story of an Armenian apostate, Garabet, who was executed publicly. Garabet, in a moment of weakness, had accepted Islam. But, repenting of his apostasy, he apostasized from Islam back to Christianity and was "executed as an apostate from Islam." [23] Berberian, an eye-witness, wrote of him as follows:

> A youth from Samatia of Armenian race named Hovagim, [24] who four months earlier was received into the Mohammedan faith and who had later become penitent, had disguised himself in European attire, and had roamed incognito. Betrayed, he was condemned to death. The Ambassador of England, Lord Canning, tried to save him from death, but the government beheaded him at the Baluk Bazaar gate of Constantinople. [25]

Berberian continues to state:

> The Empires of France and England demanded of the Sultan freedom of religion for every nation so that if an apostate should return to his faith no such violence be enforced. [26]

This martyr gave sufficient cause to the European nations represented in Constantinople to request religious liberty. With the insistence of Sir Stratford Canning, the British ambassador, and supported by the French and Prussian ministers, [27] the Sultan gave a pledge that no person would be persecuted for his religious opinions in Turkey. [28] The execution of Garabet had occurred on August 17, 1843 and the demand by the European powers was made on February 21, 1844. [29] The event had an important influence upon the cause of religious liberty in Turkey, and an important bearing upon the mission work in that country. [30] By March 21,

23. Hamlin, *op. cit.*, pp. 80-81.
24. The American missionaries had identified him as Garabet, while Berberian states the name of the martyr was Hovagim.
25. Berberian, *op. cit.*, pp. 515-516.
26. *Ibid.*, p. 518.
27. Prime adds Russian, too.
28. Dwight, *op. cit.*, pp. 157-160; Prime, *op. cit.*, p. 291; Berberian, *op. cit.*, p. 278.
29. Berberian, *op. cit.*, pp. 515-518.
30. Prime, *op. cit.*, p. 291.

1844, a written pledge had been obtained from the Sultan that effectual measures were to be taken to prevent the execution of a Christian who might be an apostate. On March 23, his personal assurance was given to Sir Stratford Canning that from then on neither Christianity was to be insulted in his dominions nor were Christians in any way to be persecuted for their religion.[31]

The Armenians had of course liked the reforms in Turkey[32] in the Western direction since it provided hope that European influence might assure a saner Turkish administration. They rejoiced, particularly, that certain elements in some European countries insisted that their Governments were "morally bound to go to the aid of what they considered to be misgoverned and maltreated subjects of the Sultan."[33] Their joy was immensely great, however, when religious freedom was secured.

Curiously, however, the Armenian Church in this same period considered the Armenian Christian who took the Bible as his sole guide to be an apostate and placed the heaviest pressure its civil power could muster. The surprise of the "regenerated" Armenians was great, therefore, that freedom of conscience in religious matters decreed by a Mohammedan Government, was not granted by the Armenian Apostolic Church on grounds that national solidarity would be endangered. This strange contradiction, in a period when the air was full of change and reform, did

31. *Ibid.*, p. 292; Hamlin, *op. cit.*, p. 82.
32. The Armenian Apostolic Church's position over against Islam was one of inarticulate rejection of Islam as a saving religion and a reluctant acceptance of the law that it may not convert Moslems by the public proclamation of the Gospel. The Mohammedan faith was the official religion of the Empire, with the Sultan as the Caliph. The same Sultan had extended the *millet* status to the Armenian Patriarch and his Christian subjects according to which the Armenians could and did practice their religion without molestation. The *millet* system had thus encouraged the concept of non-interference in each other's religious affairs and practices. Therefore, the arrangement was not conducive to proselytizing. Were the Armenian Church to attempt to make incursions upon Islam, the *millet* status and its arrangement would have been violated. Thus reluctantly, the Armenian Church had become reconciled to the situation of accepting the right to a special Christian community status and letting Islam and the Mohammedans alone. The accumulated experience of the Armenian Apostolic Church would have led them to advise the American missionaries that they would be laboring in vain to convert Mohammedans to Christianity. This same experience would have led them to advise the missionaries that their hope of reaching the Mohammedans through "regenerated" Armenians would have been equally in vain.
However, the violation of this "covenant" between the Sultan and the Armenian Church as a threat to the Armenians does not come out strongly anywhere in our research. Therefore, the opposition to the American missionaries are on the grounds that have been suggested throughout this paper. It is true, however, that Armenians in government positions would be and were sympathetic with the fears of the Porte that the missionaries might make incursions into the Mohammedan fold. Thus, these officials were in league with the government when attempts were made to oust the American missionaries out of Turkey. This cooperation would have served the cause of Armenians who were opposed to the activities of the American missionaries among the Armenians. However, since the American missionaries were not attempting any conversion of Moslems, the Armenians could not have opposed the missionaries on the political ground that their survival was being threatened.
33. Stavrinos, *op. cit.*, p. 37.

not help win the dissidents back to the Armenian Church—on the contrary, with the excommunication decrees polarizing the two groups, a separate church was finally founded. The vested powers had carried their pressure too far.

The Patriarch, as it was mentioned, could have successfully obstructed the continuation of the newly-established Evangelical Church through the authority given to him by the *Millet*[34] system of the Empire.

C. The Millet System in Turkey

In the Ottoman Empire, there developed an administrative feature in respect to Christian denominations which came to be termed the *Millet* system. The system thus denoted implies that the Sultans granted autonomy in various measure to bodies of their non-Moslem subjects who were classified according to the dignitary whom they recognized as their spiritual chief. The *Millet* of the Rum, consisted of those who obeyed the Orthodox Patriarch, the Armenian *Millet* of those spiritually subject to the Armenian Gregorian Patriarch.[35] Over the years, there came about the Uniat Armenian Church *Millet*, the Chaldean *Millet*, the Latin *Millet*, and the Jewish *Millet* with a Grand Rabbi in Istanbul.[36]

The *Millet* system was instituted by Mohammed II when he took possession of Constantinople in 1453 and found there a Greek Patriarch with spiritual jurisdiction over the whole Greek Church. He made the Patriarch responsible for the good conduct of his people, granting him at the same time with such civil powers as were necessary to enable him to maintain his authority. Following the same principle, he removed the Armenian Bishop of Broosa in 1463[37] to Constantinople and constituted

---

34. A Turkish word which means "nation" or "special community."
35. Luke, *op. cit.*, pp. 7 f.
36. *Collier's Encyclopedia, op. cit.*, p. 723.
37. Etmekjian, James, *The French Influence on the Western Armenian Renaissance* (New York: Twayne Publishers, Inc., 1964), p. 86.

him Patriarch of all Armenians in Turkey[38] with civil powers corresponding to those of the Greek Patriarch.[39]

For the Sultan, the system was a convenient way of controlling the subject peoples—that is, by holding the religious heads responsible for their conduct. On the other hand, the system was advantageous for the Patriarchs who were thus enabled to keep their national Christian membership together. Every Christian subject had to enroll in some of the existing communities, having a Patriarch as his chief.[40] Christians, thus, were organized to give obedience to their Patriarchs. The Patriarchs, on the other hand, were able to force obedience by the simple process of inflicting penalties for spiritual or civil offences. They were also able to win their obedience by alleviating burdens of oppression by representation at the Porte to reprieve the unjust acts of governors.[41] One grave disadvantage of the system for the individual Christian was that he could not detach himself from one or the other community without renouncing his civil right and privilege and exposing himself to the "consequences of complete outlawry."[42]

Advantageous as the *Millet* system was for the Armenian Patriarch, it also mitigated against the stability of the existing Armenian community because the principle of separate community status enabled other religious groups, by appropriate influence upon the Government, to

---

38. Armenians came into Cilicia (later to become part of Turkey) in the eleventh century. The kings of Ani, Van, and Kars in Armenia, unable to withstand the Seljuk attacks, retired within the limits of the Greek empire. Equally unable to withstand the doctrinal disputes and the pressures to unite with the Greek Church, Armenians finally established an independent Kingdom in the Cilician Taurus in 1080 under Rupen. This new Kingdom, which was governed by Rupen's descendents for 295 years, extended from the Taurus to the sea and the Euphrates to the western limits of Cilicia. It was terminated by the indescribable barbarities of Egypt in 1375. In 1463 when Sultan Mohammed II brought bishop Joakim of Broosa to the Metropolis "a few distinguished Armenian families" came with the bishop. Later, many more Armenians were brought and made to settle in Constantinople where bishop Joakim was given "letters patent, authorizing him to assume the spiritual jurisdiction of all the Armenians in Greece and Asia Minor." He was styled "Batrig" or "Patriarch." In due time, with the changing Sultans and the stabilization of the office of the Patriarch, the latter's position as religious and civic head became very effective and strong. The missionaries understood the importance and strength of the office of the Patriarch very accurately, and Hamlin speaks for them in the following words:

A brief note, with the patriarch's official seal stamped on it, would send any one of his people into exile or to prison . . . This gave them greater power for good, but also for evil. It gave them official access, at any time, to any member of the Divan; and their views were received as authorative with respect to their own people. They had the power to bind and to loose on earth as well as heaven. They had both spiritual and temporal power.

(See Chamchean, *op. cit.,* Vol. II, pp. 158-168, 229-230, 301-309; Smith, *Researches,* Vol. I, pp. 39-40; Hamlin, *op. cit.,* p. 131).
39. Dwight, *op. cit.,* p. 83.
40. *Ibid.,* p. 212.
41. Hamlin, *op. cit.,* p. 24.
42. Dwight, *op. cit.,* p. 212.

obtain the same rights. It was due to that very principle that in 1830, the Armenian Catholics [43] were taken out of the "jurisdiction of the Armenian Patriarchate" and placed under the jurisdiction of the head of a new Catholic *Millet*. The newly-formed community included all other Catholics who were subjects of Turkey. [44] Basing themselves on this principle of administration, the Armenian Evangelicals asked for recognition as a special community of their own.

D. The Establishment of the Protestant Millet

The Armenian Evangelicals were not able to obtain this special status on their own. The four centuries of relationship between the Porte and the Armenian Patriarchs militated against such an arrangement. There had been established a strong protocol, each side knowing the limits of its rights. As a result, the Porte would not act on a request without clearing it first with the Patriarch. Added to the matter of protocol was the fact that the Patriarchate was often modified by the power of the magnates of the community. [45] Beginning with the Greek War of Independence (1821-1829), and even earlier, Armenians began to receive recognition from the

43. Armenian contact with Roman Catholicism was established fifteen years after the founding of the Armenian Kingdom in Cilicia by Rupen I in 1080. The military and feudalistic systems of West Europe made their impact on the new kingdom. Closer contact was established when Latin feudal kings and lords married members of the Armenian princely families and Armenian princes, among them King Leo II, married Latin princesses. The Armenian court circles sometimes pressured the Armenian Apostolic Church to unite with Catholicism and many Armenians became Francophile. Despite the efforts of some Armenian kings to Latinize and achieve union with Catholicism, they were resisted by the greater majority of Armenian clergy and laymen—in some instances, princes were done away with. However, as a result of the influence of the Latin court and the work of the Latin missionaries, there developed a substantial pro-Latin and anti-Latin element. The struggle spread among the people of Cilicia and Eastern Armenia by Catholic missionaries, this work continuing through the fourteenth and fifteenth centuries. Schools were opened for Armenians even in Rome, that of Pope Gregory XIII being the more prominent one. In the seventeenth century the Catholic Church embarked upon an extensive program of missionary activity. During the period that covered the reign of Louis XIV (1643-1715), the Armenian clergy became more tolerant toward the catholic missionaries. Some clergy, among whom was the founder of an Armenian Catholic Order, Mkhitar Sepasdatsi, embraced Catholicism. Numerous efforts were made through the centuries to effect the union of the Armenian Apostolic Church with the Roman Catholic Church since the rites and liturgy of the two churches bore close resemblance. These efforts failed, but in the process many Armenians embraced Catholicism and the Uniat Armenian Catholic Church was recognized by the Pope. In Constantinople in 1830 this Church obtained a separate Armenian Roman Catholic *millet* status from the Sultan. Prior to the obtaining of that status, the Patriarch of the Armenian Apostolic Church was also the civil head of the Armenian Catholics in the Empire.

(See James Etmekjian, *op. cit.*, pp. 53-66; Jacques de Morgan, *The History of the Armenian People*, Paris, 1918. Translated from the French by E. F. Barry, Boston, Hairenik Association)

44. James Etmekjian, *op. cit.*, p. 86.

45. Dwight, *op. cit.*, p. 84.

Ottoman Government. In 1818 Sarkis and Krikor Duzoghlu were appointed superintendents of the Imperial Ottoman Bank; the Superintendent of the Powder Factory came to be Armenian; Haroutune Amira Bezjian became a trusted friend of the Sultan; other Armenians reached prominent positions during the reigns of both Sultan Mahmoud and his son Abdul-Mejid, including that of Royal Architect. [46] These men, along with others, were instrumental in electing the Patriarch to the See of Constantinople. Therefore, the combined influence of the Patriarch and the Armenians of influence at the Porte (the Amiras) made it impossible for Evangelicals to obtain the special community status they were seeking.

The Catholic example became an important point of argument before the Porte when the Armenian Evangelicals found it necessary to ask for *Millet* status. By 1847, about a year after the founding of the Armenian Evangelical Church, the Protestant *Millet* status was given to all Protestants in the Empire, but especially to the Armenian Protestants. [47] "Lord Cowley," writes Ormanian, "who was temporarily administering the English Embassy . . . *basing himself on the arrangements made for the Catholics*, requested and obtained from the Ottoman Government the right of an independent community for the Protestants." (Italics mine) [48]

Therefore, without outside pressure, the Armenian Evangelical community of the newly-found Armenian Evangelical Church would have had no civil status. The pressure was put on the Porte by Ambassadors of the European Christian nations. As Hamlin points out, "in 1847, the grand vizier, by renewed pressure, issued a firman acknowledging the new Protestant community, and according to it all the rights of other communities in the empire." [49] Sir Stratford Canning, whose influence on the Sultans commencing 1808 and ending 1858 [50] was extremely great, pressed hard for the establishment of a Protestant *Millet*. "Finally," wrote eye-witness Hamlin, "Lord Cowley, during a visit home of Sir Stratford, obtained it." [51] It was a grand stride forward for freedom of conscience. [52]

46. Etmekjian, *op. cit.*, p. 82.
47. *Ibid.*, p. 86.
48. Ormanian, *op. cit.*, p. 3805.
49. Hamlin, *op. cit.*, p. 134.
50. Luke, *op. cit.*, p. 54.
51. Hamlin, *op. cit.*, p. 134.
52. The firman of 1847, having been issued only under the ministerial authority of the Porte, was liable to be withdrawn on a change of ministry, or by imperial command. Therefore, Ambassador Stratford continued work on the question until in November, 1850, a charter was granted to the Protestants by 'His Imperial Majesty, Sultan Abdul-Mejid,' completing and confirming their distinct organization as a civil community, and securing to them equal religious rights with the older Christian organizations. . . . It secured perpetually to the Protestants the right of choosing their own head, of transacting business, of worship, of burial, free from all molestation, and promised to them protection by the imperial government against persecution. (See Prime, *op. cit.*, pp. 352-353.)

The explanations given of the turning of the Ottoman Empire to the West under Selim III, Mahmoud II, and Abdul-Mejid with a passion for reform has amply illustrated the truth that external factors played a role in creating the special Armenian Protestant *Millet*. It is the judgment of this writer that without this Ottoman trend for reform in western style, European representation would not have been so influential and effective. Consequently, the established protocol between the Porte and the Armenian Patriarchate would not have been broken and the obtaining of special status for the Armenian Evangelicals would not have been possible. By the same token, because of the favor with which Turkey looked upon Western representation, the Ambassadors of the European Christian nations were able to bring their influence to bear on the obtaining of rights for this other developing minority group, namely, the Armenian Protestants. Without the sympathetic understanding of the European Ambassadors and their specific assistance in the cause of obtaining such a special status, the Armenian Patriarchate, this author believes, would have been able to prevent the granting of such a status. This is not to say that the Armenian Patriarchate would have been right to obstruct the establishment of a Protestant *Millet*. It is simply to state that the Patriarchate was inflexible enough to prevent such a development.

Historical events do not rise out of a vacuum. The establishment of a separate Armenian Protestant *Millet* did not arise out of a vacuum either. It came about because there was the right amount of mixture of stimulation for reform, sufficient amount of desire for freedom from frustration and hopelessness, the necessary strength of presence in the persons of the American missionaries to provide a vision for Armenian dreams, and the exact amount of foreign influence to bring about the event. Further, the admixtures were closely knit with the spirit of the times. The special status was possible because of what the nineteenth century was: a time of ferment, with the influence of the American and French Revolutions only gradually reaching and making their impact on the subjects of the backward Ottoman Empire; a time of revitalization, with the influence of missionary zeal penetrating many spheres of the world but in Turkey the hearts of Armenians. Out of all these, as yarns that knitters use, first was knit the event of the founding of the Armenian Evangelical Church, and next the establishment of the special community with similar rights as other recognized *millets* possessed.

The establishment of the special Armenian Protestant Community was unfortunate because it had its detriments. The small minority continued to be exposed to social ostracism, ridicule, insults, business boycotts for a long time. The separation disrupted family solidarity, for there came about alienation between relatives—sometimes between parent and son, brother and sister. The separation also weakened to some extent the solidarity of the Armenian people as a whole. The Reverend S.K. Sulahian, presenting the thinking of Dr. M.S. Kaprielian out of the latter's *Armenian Protestantism—Its Past and Future*, states that the separated Protestant Community became a hindrance to the reformation of the Armenian Apostolic Church. "Whenever, thereafter, there was any inclination for reform within the church," he writes, "there was a reluctance, delay or outright refusal because of fear that it might mean an admission that the Evangelicals were right. Any tendency towards reform was subject to suspicion as Protestant."[53]

On the other hand, the refusal of the Armenian Church to cooperate with the "regenerated" was even more unfortunate. The Church lost a good opportunity not only to introduce healthy reforms into its structure, but also lost a great opportunity to educate and thus enlighten the citizens of Turkey when it failed to cooperate with the American missionaries and the "reformed" Armenians. The Church, if it had cooperated fully with the American missionaries, might have enlightened the populace by education through a wide system of schools.[54] An excellent system was already in practice, the Lancastrian System of Schools,[55] which was also popular as a new educational phenomenon in England, United States, Venezuela and Canada.

It may be argued that it is unrealistic to expect that Turks would have wanted to take advantage of education offered by Christians. Yet, evidence exists that by 1914 thousands of Turks were taking advantage of such education. Author Strong believes that Armenians would have had an important effect on structuring Turkey if the entire nation had participated in Church reform and created a contagion for education in mid-

53. The Armenian Evangelical Union of America, *The One Hundred and Twenty-fifth Anniversary of the Armenian Evangelical Movement* (1846-1971) (New York: Papken Kadehjian Press, 1971), p. 23.

54. It is not valid to argue for the historical past in "ifs." Just the same, it is edifying to consider possibilities that might have produced great results. If we were to take into account that a Protestant Community of 50,900 (Supra p. 92, footnote 70) or just two percent of the 2-1/2 million Armenian population in occupied Cilicia, could produce 369 primary schools and 850 teachers by 1914, the remaining ninety-eight percent could have founded 18,081 such schools and given 41,650 teachers. A census in Turkey records that there were 17,500 Government primary schools and 42,000 teachers in the country in 1955. (See Collier's Encyclopedia, op. cit., p. 725). It is obvious that a great contribution could have been made towards literacy in Turkey if the combined energies of the mission and the Armenian Church had been directed towards that end. This writer wants to repeat his acknowledgment of the inadequacy of this form of estimating. Yet, the contrast, made in extreme form, might help the realization that a great opportunity was lost to structure Turkey. Further, had such an educational system been in operation it would have structured Turkey in terms of a culture which had Christian foundation. Might not Turkey have been on the side of the Allies as a result in 1914? If so, the genocide of the Armenians might not have occurred. If the Church had operated on the Christian principle that he who loses his soul finds it, trends might have changed.

55. Supra, p. 29, footnote 29.

nineteenth century which was experienced by Turkey in the early twentieth century. Speaking for the twentieth century, author Strong presents the following picture:

> At once all schools, higher and lower, became crowded, Mohammedan youth pressing in with the Armenian. A high Turkish official, speaking to a throng of Armenians on the steps of Euphrates College at Harpoot, said: 'Hitherto only Armenians have been able to avail themselves of the privileges of this college. We Turks have been forbidden to send our children here. That is all changed now and we will share with you in the enjoyment of what this institution offers to all who come within its doors.' Now governors even sought advice and help of missionaries and of Armenian leaders in political and educational matters.[56]

In a moment of insight, the President of the Armenian National Council had said to Dwight in the 1860's:

> Now is the time for you to work for the Armenian people. Such an opportunity as you now enjoy may soon pass away and never more return. You should greatly enlarge your operations. Where you have one missionary, you should have ten; and where you have one book, you should put ten books in circulation.[57]

It is a pity that he did not address himself to the Patriarchate and say that it was time to work with the missionaries because such an opportunity would never return. He might have added: "Perchance we might be instrumental in exciting the interest of the entire Turkish population and in so doing enlighten their minds and souls." The tragic truth appears to be that there was no "dream" on the part of the Armenian Church to develop a concern for Turkey itself. Had the Armenian Church awakened to its responsibility and seen the unusual opportunity it had of helping elevate Turkey's education and culture, the Lancastrian System could have been successfully applied universally to help reduce the high incidence of illiteracy in the Ottoman Empire. If, instead of making the preservation of the Armenian Church and Armenian people the supreme goal, the spiritual leadership had demonstrated service arising out of love and concern, the response of Government and people might have been more charitable towards the Armenians. When it is observed that there has never been a charitable institution founded by the Armenian Church for the *strict benefit* of the Muslim population, the lack of vision for Turkey is made evident. The Church had no program of social or humanitarian action, had made no effort to enlighten illiterate Turkey, nor had it tried to demonstrate love for the Turkish populace by providing avenues of

---

56. Strong, *op. cit.*, p. 409.
57. *Ibid.*, p. 197.

charitable service. Many individual Armenians had served both Government and Empire valiantly and helpfully. But the Church, as the instrument of God's love, had not gone out of that same love to heal and serve others except Armenians. One would not be wrong to state that love and concern would have endeared the Armenian people in the eyes of the Turkish leaders and population. There are instances in history when a conquered people have conquered the conquerors with their depth of love, concern and spirituality.

What could the Armenian Chuch have done? Much,[58] if it had been open to Christ's call in a serious way 'to love one's neighbor as oneself.' Being open in this sense, however, would have implied a deep and revolutionary evaluation of the mission of the Church—a deep understanding of the meaning of Jesus of Nazareth. This evaluation was not made and the deeper understanding was lacking.

In summarizing the argument of this work, this researcher desires to hold to the conviction that each cause in itself would not have brought on a separation, but that *all the causes cumulatively* led to the schism. If we grant the right to associations for missionary endeavors, and we should, then we have to accept that without the missionary preaching and training the existent Armenian openness to change the condition of the Armenian Church might not have been stimulated to the extent of a radical demand for "regenerated" individuals and a "regenerated" Armenian Church. On the other hand, if it weren't for the unbending, non-compromising attitude of the Armenian Church for reasons of its own, whether valid or not, a solution might have been found to reduce the stress of the "regenerated." It is conceivable, for instance, that a "low" Anglican type of a church might have been acceptable wherein the theology could have been of the "protestant" kind and the "establishment" a milder form of a hierarchy. Further, were it not for the strong, active, aggressive and judgmental zeal and activity of the "awakened," the Armenian Church might have been able to endure the milder activities of the missionaries and the "regenerated." Finally, because of the rights the Patriarch had from the Ottoman Government over his subjects, it was possible for the Patriarch to quash the movement. The presence and influence in Constantinople, however, of the representatives of European powers in a nineteenth-century reform-oriented Turkey neutralized the Patriarch's historic authority. This presence, further, would not have been effective were it not for the fact that Turkey had weakened and was turning to the West for assistance to strengthen itself. This researcher, therefore, cannot concede that there was any one party to blame for the separation. All

58. See H. A. Chakmakjian, *op. cit.,* p. 129 for suggestions of what the Church could have done.

things worked together to bring it about. This writer believes that the realization that there was not one party to blame, but it was the inevitable result of historical events on which no one had any control, would introduce a healthy outlook wherein the two traditions, namely the Armenian Apostolic and the Armenian Evangelical, could put their intellectual and spiritual prowess at work to engage in ecumenical conversations for the good of all and the glory of God's Kingdom.

It was a great pity that the unique opportunity was not exploited then. It will be tragic if a united and concerted effort for the Christian edification of the Armenians and their neighbors, wherever they may be, is not practiced now.

CHAPTER X

CONCLUSION

A. *Secession Need not Have Been Feared*

In the longer perspective of history, the fears of the Armenian Church authorities that the success of the American mission would break up the unity of the National Church and loosen the loyalty of Armenians to the nation turned out to be unfounded. The Armenian Evangelicals remained patriotic Armenians, for, as Yeghia S. Kassouny testifies "Armenian Evangelicals are just as pure and patriotic Armenians as are the Gregorian Armenians."[1] Conversion to a reform (evangelical) point of view did not spell the abandonment of national identity—a condition which is deplored by H.A. Chakmakjian,[2] but which the founding fathers said would not happen.[3] In a less emphatic way His Grace Archbishop Hrant Khatchadourian, prelate of the Prelacy of the Armenian Apostolic Church of America, confirms the testimony of Y.S. Kassouny. In response to a request by the writer of this dissertation for a frank evaluation of the Armenian Protestant Movement, Archbishop Khatchadourian states that "the love of foreigners" was stressed by those who had embraced Protestantism. However, he continues to point out the following:

> But, in course of time, specially in the last thirty years, a return to the Armenian stamp and national expression is observable. This reality is specially noticeable among the Armenian Protestant communities in the Middle East.
> Here, we wish to remember with commendation, however, that from the very beginning individuals and protestant ministers were found who constantly tried to keep alive the Armenian ethos through their sermons and activities.[4]

The Evangelical Movement was not as tragic as the Armenian Church assumed it would be; in fact the Movement made some important

---

1. Kassouny, *Loossashavigh*, p. 66.
2. H.A. Chakmakjian, *op. cit.*, pp. 126-127, where he writes: "However genuinely spiritual were the motives of the Armenian Protestant forefathers, still, they too, were dominated by the nationalistic outlook, from a religious angle. The *name* they chose for the first church, persisting to our day, amply indicates this. It was Christened 'the Evangelical Church of Armenia,' in contrast with the 'Holy Apostolic Church of Armenia.' And there is ample ground to confess that *Armenia* was stressed as much as *Evangelical . . .* it was a localized and national longing rather than a longing for the regeneration of Armenians as well as non-Armenians."
3. Eutudjian, *op. cit.*, p. 167.
4. Letter of Archbishop Hrant Khatchadourian dated January 28, 1970.

contributions to Armenian life. In the *first* place, the concept of the spirit of religious toleration was eventually accepted. The time came when bishops condescended to preach from Armenian Evangelical pulpits, when invited, and permitted Evangelical pastors to return the compliment. In the *second* place, "The religious, educational, and social life of the Armenian nation has been leavened by the influence of this spiritual movement."[5] In the *third* place, the Evangelicals, with the assistance of the missionaries, created an enviable system of education from kindergarten to college from which, gradually, large numbers of Armenian Apostolic children benefited,[6] with the additional benefit of creating Armenian Apostolic competition.[7] The *fourth* major contribution was the translation as well as the popularization of the Bible, which achievement, Orchanian concedes, also helped purify the spoken language.[8] In the *fifth* place, the Evangelicals influenced the introduction of a Sunday School system into the Apostolic Church.[9] In the *sixth* place, the Evangelicals managed to keep church and politics separate and were able to have a place in the church for men and women of all political views—thus mediating against divisiveness, a condition which is praised by the Armenian Apostolics who are plagued with serious divisive conflicts.[10] A *seventh* important contribution was the influence of the Evangelicals to keep the Apostolic community open to reform or to lead to a Roman Catholic type of counter-reformation. A.A. Bedikian, believing this influence to have brought the Armenian Apostolic Church closer to the Evangelicals, writes that the same "Evangelicalism that the Mother Church could not contain or tolerate over a century ago, is not only

5.   Chakmakjian, H.A., *op. cit.*, p. 125.
6.   The system was wrecked in 1915 with the commencement of the massacres, but by 1920 it was re-established in Lebanon and Syria where the bulk of the Armenian 'remnants' settled. By the founding of the Haigazian College in Beirut in 1955, the only degree-giving institution among Armenians outside Soviet Armenia, the higher education end of the system was added. Interestingly, this college has to date given two Bachelor of Art degrees to two Armenian celibate priests of the Apostolic Church. Attendance in Evangelical Schools up to high school is about 79% Apostolic and 21% Protestant and other, such as Catholic and Arab.
7.   Kherlopian, *op. cit.*, pp. 17-19.
8.   K. Orchanian, *History of the Armenian Language and Linguistics* (Marsovan: Nerso and Srabian, 1913), pp. 114-115.
9.   G. Chopourian, *Our Armenian Christian Heritage*, published by the Armenian Evangelical Union of America, Eastern States and Canada (Philadelphia: Ideal Press, Inc., 1962), p. 111.
10.   This separation of church and politics, within the church community, is similar to the separation of Church and State within the United States. In all probability, American congregational polity had provided this direction to the Armenian Evangelical.

tolerated but cultivated and cherished at the present time."[11] An *eighth* influence, though touched upon lightly under the third influence listed, must receive greater attention. A fair evaluation of the educational activities of the Armenian Protestants will demonstrate that the Armenian nation, on the whole, was stimulated to competition in the founding of new and the improving of old schools to the extent that some Protestants are beginning to state today that the Armenian Apostolic Schools are getting ahead of the Protestant ones. A situation which, if valid, gives nothing but joy and deep satisfaction to the Armenian Protestant. The *ninth* influence, though a literary one, is most important. It has to do with the purification of the spoken Armenian language of the nineteenth century. K. Orchanian concedes, for instance, that the translation of the Scriptures into the vernacular Armenian helped purify the spoken Armenian language of the time.[12] The spoken language, put into writing in a book as important as the Bible, developed a uniform Armenian vernacular and helped systematize grammatical constructions. In the *tenth* and final place, Evangelicalism provided a haven to those who had imbibed agnostic views during their intellectual training. Many had imbibed, with the good, the concepts of "infidelity" of France and the agnosticism of Voltaire who had "emptied the religious concept of nearly all its content and made God an unknowable Supreme Being, remote originator and guarantor of an orderly universe and moral law."[13] The Armenian Evangelical Movement, with its criticism of the ceremonial and sacerdotal in the Armenian Church, became a haven to a number who had become critical of the worse aspects of the Church. Therefore, as a result of the Evangelical stand, instead of turning totally agnostic, or forming a reform group of more radical nature, a number were able to enter more readily into the religious movement in which "living according to the dictates of Jesus" was acceptable to them. Without this escape valve, it is feared that the Armenian Apostolic Church would have found itself face to face with a more dangerous and radical resistance or it would have lost to agnosticism a great number of its learned men.

B. Higher Clergy Acknowledge the Value
of the Movement

Three "princes" of the Armenian Apostolic Church have stated, with

11. A.A. Bedikian, *The Rise of the Evangelical Movement Among Armenians* (New York: Armenian Missionary Association of America, 1970) p. 4 (Being an English translation of the Armenian entitled, *The Beginnings of the Evangelical Movement Among Armenians*. New York: Armenian Missionary Association of America, 1964).

12. K. Orchanian, *op. cit.,* pp. 114-115.

13. Collier's Encyclopedia, *op. cit.,* Article, "Voltaire" by Herbert Dieckmann, p. 297.

certain reservations, that the Protestant movement has contributed to the spiritual well-being of the people. The first one is His Grace, Bishop Papken Varjabedian, former prelate of the Diocese of California of the Armenian Church. When he came to Philadelphia in the early 1960's, this writer paid a courtesy visit to him. During the conversation that followed, he pointed out thoughtfully that the Armenian Evangelicals had popularized the Bible and the Sunday School, and had developed exemplary schools. His Grace, Archbishop Hrant Khatchadourian, upon request for evaluation of the Protestant movement, wrote the following message:

> Overlooking some of its negative characteristics or realities, Armenian Protestantism however, considered from a broad point of view, generally speaking brought some blessings in the circle of the Armenian people and the Armenian Church. These were a general feeling of love of religion, love of Bible-reading, a prayerful life, higher education and the Sunday School movement. . . . These are the non-objectionable blessings of Armenian Protestantism beginning from the days of its origin generally until our days. [14]

The third Churchman to be contacted was His Grace Archbishop Torkom Manoogian of the Diocese of the Armenian Church of America. [15] After stating, in an undated but signed statement, that the Protestant Missionary movement among already Christian Armenians in Turkey was an imposition and not a genuine movement of reformation from within the Armenian Church he enumerates the positive results as follows:

> A keen awareness was alerted toward basic needs of human soul, namely, education and spiritual nourishment. Renewed attempts were made to update the knowledge of the church members and to affirm the bases for their Christian beliefs. Catechetical textbooks and religious magazines were published; new seminaries were established for the training of clergy; the importance of preaching the Word was emphasized by reiterating the special education of preachers; the traditional customs of family prayer, bible reading and other devotional practices were encouraged. [16]

C. What of the Future?

In the light of acknowledgments that the movement has had its value,

---

14. Letter dated January 28, 1970.
15. There are two diocesan centers in the United States. The Diocese of the Armenian Church of America is located at 630 Second Avenue, New York City, and represents the See of Etchmiadzin. The See of Cilicia located at Antelias, Lebanon is represented by the Prelacy of the Armenian Apostolic Church of America, 777 United Nations Plaza, New York City.
16. A signed statement by Archbishop Torkom Manoogian, 1970.

one wonders if there is hope for some "reform" within the Armenian Church to be followed by some cooperative plans for union or concerted action.

If H.F.B. Lynch's estimate of the lesson taught by history is correct, the future does not hold hope for a united effort. At the end of his 88-page lengthy chapter on "Edgmiatsin and the Armenian Church" Lynch concludes:

> On the other hand, the lesson which is taught by history is that no nation and no Christianity will succeed with the Armenians which endeavours to deflect them from their own opinions and to preclude them from working out their own salvation in their own way.[17]

As one surveys the present scene, one is faced with both hope and despair. In his *The Armenian Church* [18] Catholicos Papken Gulesserian, progressive and influential as he was, rejected the proposal of an anonymous book [19] written in 1866 for some mild reforms. The *Image of the Holy Gregorian Church of Armenia* proposed changes in the Creed, Prayerbook, and Liturgy, a major one being the removal of all references to the *mediation of saints*. [20] The *Image* was summarily condemned by the Patriarchate in Constantinople on the assumption that those propagating it were influenced by the Protestant movement "whose originators, the American missionaries, had ignorantly criticized the Armenian Church."[21] Gulesserian, too, dismisses the book as impractical and unacceptable.

However, in the last decade or so, strong voices have been heard for "renewal" and "reform." In the October, 1958 issue of *The Armenian Guardian* [22] the editor wrote on the basic cause of the turmoil in the Armenian Church and found it to be in the nationalism of the Armenian people. He considered it to be logical that the nationalistic understanding of the Armenian Church be uprooted—by which he understood the stoppage of the use of the Church for the preservation of the Armenian

17. H.F.B. Lynch, *Armenia: Travels and Studies*. In Two volumes. (New York: Longmans, Green, and Co., 1901), p. 314.
18. Papken Gulesserian, *The Armenian Church* (Jerusalem: St. James Printing Press, 1930).
19. *Image of the Holy Gregorian Church of Armenia*, Anonymous (Cited in Gulesserian, *op. cit.*, pp. 2-7).
20. *Ibid.*
21. *Ibid.*, p. 7.
22. *The Armenian Guardian*, A monthly publication of the youth of the Diocese of the Armenian Church of America (New York: October, 1958).

language. [23] The more radical demand for reform came over the Labor Day week-end in 1968. At that time, the Armenian Christian Youth Organization of America was assembled at Williams Bay, Wisconsin, for their General Assembly. There, a new spirit was born, as embodied in a document which was presented at the last session of the Assembly and was subsequently dubbed the "Williams Bay Manifesto." [24] The Manifesto began by stating that "the world is in an age of revolution" and that to be relevant the Church must "speak of God's will in terms of today." It continued to say that the youth of the Armenian Church are disturbed by the "church's refusal to be part of the twentieth century" in finding solutions to the real problems of the day and that it concerned itself mainly with "erecting costly buildings and monuments and amassing material goods, rationalizing that this is necessary for self-preservation." Stating that "in the minds of many Armenians the Armenian Church's primary function is to act as the defender of nationalism" the manifesto cast forth the following challenge in the last paragraph:

The time has come when we, the youth of the Armenian Church, can no longer in conscience allow ourselves to be used as instruments for the preservation of a church which is living in the archaic past. We feel we must make known our discontent with the present antiquated and meaningless structures and institutions and our desire to ameliorate the stagnated condition of the church which is ours. . . . We are committed to action . . . the watchword is revolution. Our revolutionary commitment and action addresses itself to a radical concern of making Christ live and grow in our church and members. We are resolved to speak out and act in accordance with the dictates of our conscience in all areas of life within and without our church, wherever Christ is being crucified anew. [25]

To the call of the youth a maturer voice was added in 1969, namely that of Professor V.L. Parsegian. [26] The occasion that led him to write extensively in the Armenian newspapers asking for consideration of reforms was the controversy that arose over the marriage of the celibate priest

---

23. *Ibid.*
24. Reported in *The Armenian Church,* a publication of the Diocese of the Armenian Church of America (New York: November, 1968), Vol. X, No. 6, pp. 1,3. The Manifesto was given enthusiastic reception by the delegates, but its adoption was tabled pending further consideration. It was signed by seven of the eight Central Council members and twenty-nine of the fifty delegates.
25. *Ibid.*
26. Professor in the field of Atomic Physics at the Rennselaer Polytechnic Institute, Troy, New York.

(Vartabet) Kalaydjian. [27] Pointing out that "controversy threatens to weaken the Church," Parsegian said he would like to see orderly processes initiated to place the celibacy and other church issues in proper perspective *with the help of laymen*. [28] Dr. Parsegian urged His Holiness the Catholicos at Etchmiadzin and the Primates that the following matters be studied by special study groups and their recommendations become the basis for the Bishop's Council in Etchmiadzin in 1972: 1) celibacy; 2) modernization of the service of the mass; 3) organizational and administrative functions of the Church; 4) education and scholarly activities of the clergy; 5) church school and young people's programs. [29] He concluded: "We cannot permit loss of these values and weakening of the Church by unnecessary clinging to man-made rules of the past. It is timely to transform the present confusion into an effort to bring fresh attitudes and spiritual strength to the Church and to our people." [30]

Recently, a slight hope was aroused as a result of the instruction of the Catholicos of Etchmiadzin to Archbishop Torkom Manoogian of the Diocese of the Armenian Church to provide an opportunity for Armenian Evangelical pastors to meet with appointed clergy of the Diocese in order to converse on the possibility of developing some cooperation together. [31]

These are all very good signs. Unfortunately, however, there is resistance [32] to calls for reform of a fundamental nature. For instance, a strong negative response was given to the Williams Bay Manifesto by one of the major Armenian daily newspapers, the *HAIRENIK*. In five editorials the editor condemned the "new spirit" calling for the revision and traditions of the Armenian Church to be a "sickly attitude" and

---

27.   Vartabed Kalaydjian asked release from his celibate vows to get married but at the same time to be permitted to serve the church as a priest. Archbishop Torkom Manoogian, prelate of the Diocese of the Armenian Church of America permitted it. This raised afresh the past issues of celibacy and its canonical foundation or lack of it, as well as the administrative right of the prelate vis-a-vis his superior at Etchmiadzin, His Holiness Catholicos Vasken I. The issue was hotly discussed in the papers. The newspaper articles attacked the Archbishop for his audacity in going over the head of the Catholicos, while, curiously, granting the principle of the need for reform in the celibate question.

28.   The Armenian Reporter, New York, January 15, 1970, p. 7.

29.   *Ibid.*

30.   *Ibid.*

31.   This writer was invited to participate in the consultative discussions.

32.   The most recent setback to the Armenian Church was the resignation of the former Bishop Vasken Kebreslian as Vicar General of the Diocese of the Armenian Church and the renunciation of his clerical order. His letter was dated January 30, 1970, and was effective as of February 15, 1970. As reported in *The Armenian Reporter* of Thursday, February 26, 1970, his decision was prompted by his resentment against the prevailing condition within the Armenian Church, a condition which is characterized with its unchanging attitudes toward present day needs of the Armenian people. (*The Armenian Reporter*, February 26, 1970), pp. 1,3.

proposed that "THE IMPORTANT THING IS THE RECOGNITION OF OUR SPECIAL CONDITIONS AND NEEDS AND THE UNADULTERATED PRESERVATION OF OUR NATIONAL CHARACTER."[33]

The underlying hope of this survey has been that the causes, as interpreted, might lead to a deeper as well as non-polemical understanding of the Armenian Evangelical Movement. It is believed that an understanding of the mistakes of the past, as well as the opportunities lost, might provide valuable insights for a fuller cooperation between the two groups and for an ecumenical ministry. If the two separate bodies would consider the *fundamental cause* of the separation to have been due to the *cumulative effect of unavoidable sundry factors cast in a historical frame*, they could avoid a repetition of moving in independent directions. If the two traditions could accept, as a result, that the separation was both the judgment of God and His grace, they could find avenues of cooperation which might make them a power in God's Kingdom, realizing that there is an unfinished task of mission ahead for all Christians. After all, progress is never an unhindered movement. The history of the Christian Church, within all of its various branches, has never moved forward without great difficulties. What needs to be done is to submit all divisive tendencies to the light of God's will and learn to labor within the context of the day-by-day occurences with appropriate adjustments to changing situations. Troeltsch, in the closing passage of his intensive research, speaks for this writer too when he concludes:

> One of the most serious and important truths which emerge as a result of this inquiry is this: every idea is still faced by brutal facts, and all upward movement is checked and hindered by interior and exterior difficulties. Nowhere does there exist an absolute Christian ethic, which only awaits discovery; all that we can do is to learn to control the world-situation in its successive phases just as the earlier Christian ethic did in its own way. There is also no absolute ethical transformation of material nature or of human nature; all that does exist is a constant wrestling with the problems which they raise. Thus the Christian ethic of the present day and of the future will also only be an adjustment to the world-situation, and it will only desire to achieve that which is practically possible. This is the cause of that ceaseless tension which drives man onward yet gives him the sense that he can never realize his ethical ideal. Only doctrinaire idealists or religious fanatics can fail to recognize these facts. Faith is the source of energy in the struggle of life, but life still remains a battle which is continually renewed upon ever new fronts. For every threatening abyss which is closed, another yawning gulf appears. The truth is—and this is the conclusion of the whole

---

33. *Hairenik* (Boston: Hairenik Publication Co., 1968), Oct. 26, Nov. 7, 9, 10, 13, page 1 editorials.

matter—the Kingdom of God is within us. But we must let our light shine before men in confident and untiring labour that they may see our good works and praise our Father in Heaven. The final ends of all humanity are hidden within His hands.[34]

May God deliver us from fanaticism and open before us a genuine openness to the leading of the Holy Spirit to enable us to know *truth* but express our *convictions in love.*

34. Troeltsch, *op. cit.*, p. 1013.

APPENDIX

CHRONOLOGICAL TABLE

ACCESSION DATES	CATHOLICI	PATRIARCHS	SULTANS
Aug. 23, 1808	----	----	Mahmoud II
Sept. 2, 1809	Ephraim	----	----
Dec. 27, 1815	----	Paul	----
Nov. 8, 1823	----	Garabed	-----
Sept. 16, 1831	----	Stepan the "Dove"	----
Mar. 14, 1833	John	----	----
Mar. 25, 1839	----	Hagopos	----
July 1, 1839	----	----	Abdul Medjid
Sept. 27, 1840	----	Stepan the "Dove" (Restored)	----
Oct. 1, 1841	----	Asdvadzadour	----
June 27, 1843	Nerses	----	----
July 13, 1844	----	Matteos Choohajian	----
Oct. 19, 1848	----	Hagopos (Restored)	----
Aug. 23, 1858	Matteos Choohajian	----	----
Oct. 19, 1858	----	Krikor	----
May 3, 1860	----	Sarkis	----

PAPER OF RECANTATION*

"Our most Honourable and Spiritual Father:

"Having been, by God's special Providence, born in the holy and spotless Christian religion, and particularly having been nourished in the Catholic doctrines of the holy Armenian Church, with whatever honour and love we may shew filial obedience to the same holy Church, still it is evident that for such distinguished favours we can never make a sufficient return. But alas! that being deceived by the wicked enticements of Satan, besides being found wanting in our duty, we separated from the spotless bosom of the same holy Church, and rejecting her apostolic, sound and saving doctrine, we were caught in the loose and soul-destroying doctrines of the New Sectaries. And thus we not only despised our immaculate Mother, the Holy Church, who regenerated us by the holy laver to be the sons of God, but we were also found opposers of the infallible command of Christ Jesus, who has given to his holy Church, the power of being invincible to the gates of hell. We have also sinned against the mighty power of the Holy Spirit, who guides the Church of Christ ever to remain in infallible truth; and finally we have lightly esteemed the free grace of God the Father, who was pleased to create us in this holy faith, as the single and only means of becoming the heirs of his glory.

"Behold, we were lovingly joined to this impious sect, and until now, we wilfully remained obstinate in this error. But when the holy Church, by the God-given power of your high priesthood, after having again and again resorted to counsel, and the means necessary to correct us, brandished her two-edged and Christ-given sword, which pierceth even to the dividing asunder of soul and spirit, of the joints and marrow, immediately the bands of our soul were broken, and the stupor which reigned over our hearts, dispelled; the obstinacy of our wills relaxed, we awoke from our beastly Nebuchadnezzar-like irrationality, and became aware that what we had done was against the Divine power, and that the preaching of *those deceiving* New Sectaries, which we had heartily received, was nothing else but an invention of arrogance, a snare of Satan, a sect of confusion, a broad road which leadeth to destruction.

*It is written from the mouth of those who recant, and is addressed to the Patriarch.

136

"Wherefore, repenting of these our impious deeds, of our own will and choice we have fled again to the bosom of our immaculate and holy Armenian Church; and, in order to excite her gracious compassion towards us, receiving your Spiritual and Christian authority as our Mediator, we cry, 'Father, we have sinned against Heaven and before thee,' in order that she may grant us forgiveness with a forgetful indulgence towards our former dissolute lives; and whatever penance she may impose we will willingly perform; and we confess that the faith of the holy Church is spotless, her sacraments Divine, her rites of apostolic origin, her ritual pious. And whatever this same holy Church receiveth, whether it be a matter of faith or ceremony, we also receive; and whatever doctrines she rejects, we also like her reject with anathemas. And this truth, which we here express by word and letter, we also confess with our heart and mind, before the heart-searching God. And if by cherishing in our hearts something different from what we here assert, we design to deceive the holy Church by practising hypocrisy, then may we be regarded as partakers of the sin, and liable to the punishment of Ananias and Sapphira, who lied to the Holy Ghost, the fountain of truth.

"And if through fear, or for temporal advantage, or in order not to give up our own opinions, after now making this confession, we return to our former impious way, and to the error of those accursed New Sectaries, and visit them, or those like them, or have any intercourse whatever with them; then, even though we should repent, let punishment *spiritual* and *temporal* be immediately executed upon us.

"And now, in order to demonstrate that we receive with all our hearts everything we have confessed, we now sign and affix our seals each with his own hand,—once haters, but now, by the grace of God, penitent children of the holy and catholic Armenian Church."[1]

---

1. Dwight, *op. cit.*, pp. 327-329 (for the English wording); Eutudjian, *op. cit.*, pp. 153-155 (for the Armenian wording).

THE PATRIARCH'S "NEW CREED"

1. "Do you confess and receive, that faith alone cannot save a man; but with faith there must also be good works; and that not good works, but the making of a confession in accordance with the belief of the universal Church, is the sign that a Christian has the true faith?"

2. "Do you confess and receive, that the Church of Christ in this world is the visible company of believers, confessing and not concealing their faith, and is called The Church Militant, and that the head of that Holy Church is Christ, and that it is governed by the guidance of the Holy Spirit (i.e., its governors act under the influence of the Holy Spirit—Tr.), and will never cease nor fail to the end of time; it has never erred and never can err; and that there is not a single truth in the Holy Scriptures which is not acknowledged by the holy Church?"

3. "Do you confess and receive the seven Sacraments of the Church, which are Baptism, Confirmation, Penance, Communion, Ordination, Matrimony, and Extreme Unction; and that those Sacraments cannot be administered by any private Christian, but only by a regularly ordained Catholicos, or bishop, or priest, who alone has authority to administer them, and that authority they have received from Christ, through him who ordained them?"

4. "Do you confess and receive, that man, in order to be an heir of eternal salvation, must be baptized; that while unbaptized he is out of the church, and *has no salvation, even though he had never sinned at all*; likewise that until he confesses his sins, with every single circumstance, and with perfect repentance, before a priest, and submits to the penance imposed by the priest, he cannot receive the forgiveness of his sins and absolution, nor become worthy of eternal glory. Nay, if he has confessed, and should die before performing the penance, or in light and involuntary sins after confession, the soul of such, by *the prayer of the Church*, by the *deathless sacrifice* (of the mass), and by *special alms*, is purified and becomes worthy of eternal glory?"

5. "Do you confess and receive, that the mystery of the Holy Communion is the true body and blood of Christ, and that whoever does not partake of the Communion in this belief is under eternal condemnation?"

6. "Do you confess and receive that the Holy Virgin Mary, having brought forth Christ-God, is the mother of God, and that both at the time of his birth, and afterwards, her virginity remained unimpaired, that she is ever virgin, and worthy of honor above all the saints; and that the holy

wooden cross, having been stained by the Divine blood of Christ, and other holy and anointed crosses, on account of *being the image* of this, are worthy of adoration. Likewise, that the intercession of the saints is acceptable to God, and their relics and anointed pictures worthy of honor, and that God always works miracles by means both of the holy cross and holy relics?"

7. "Do you confess and receive, that to believe in the Church, means, to believe those things which the universal Holy Church unitedly believes, and to believe them in the same way she does?

"Do you thus believe the Holy Church, and do you honor and promise to keep and perform her external ceremonies of piety and Christian rites, and all her requirements, as having been received by tradition from the holy apostles, and the holy fathers who succeeded them?"

8. "Do you confess and receive, that in the Holy Church there are different offices and grades of authority successively rising, as reader, deacon, priest, bishop, catholicos; and that the catholicoses and patriarchs of every nation are Christ's viceregents, to rule the Holy Church, and govern her in due order; but should the life of one of these shepherds be vicious, the church governed by him does not thereby err in the least, and no blot comes upon the universal Church?"

9. "Do you anathematize and withdraw from that man and that society who preaches that error has entered into the faith unitedly received by the universal church, saying that the Holy Spirit has taught me so, and thus represents his own instigating spirit of error as God the Holy Spirit, and 'trusting to that, calls the Holy Mother of God the mother of Christ, and denies her perpetual virginity, and esteeming the worship offered to the Holy Cross, and the honour paid to the relics of saints, and to anointed pictures, and the reception of the intercession of the saints with God, as idolatry, calls Christ's Holy Church idolatrous, and rejects her ceremonies of piety, and all her requisitions, as superstitious, and limits God's infinite power by not receiving his working of miracles?' (See 6.) The followers of such error do you anathematize, reject, and altogether withdraw from, as impious blasphemers of the Holy Spirit, and enemies of God and all his saints?"

"These nine are the articles of faith of the Armenian Church, which every Armenian is bound to receive.

"Of the above questions, whatever truths are found in them to be confessed and acknowledged, I profess and acknowledge, and believe them all, in accordance with the Holy Church; and whatever is to be rejected and anathematized, and cast away as error and ungodliness, I reject, and anathematize, and cast away; and I believe that the Holy Catholic Church is the only pillar and ground of the truth, and whoever is out of the Church is not an heir of salvation. Feb. 4, 1846." (O.S.)[1]

1. Dwight, *op. cit.*, pp. 329-331.

LETTER OF THE
PERSECUTED CHRISTIANS TO
PATRIARCH MATTEOS CHOOHAJIAN[1]

Most Reverend and Holy Father:

The persecutions, hardships, false accusations and the harm these have caused us these days have forced us to express our protest to your Highness and Holiness. To whom can we go but to our Beloved People, who, considering us enemies, have deprived us of the church and our privileges as members? Since we are now being considered to be unbelievers and heretics and you are exercising your right to anathematize us, we in turn feel obliged to profess that we are true believers of the Church of Christ by stating our orthodox Christian beliefs.

We believe and profess the Holy Trinity, One God, the Father, the Son and the Holy Ghost—one authority, one will and one government.

We believe that our Lord Jesus Christ is perfect God and perfect man, and we confess him as the only Savior of the world and the true High Priest, Mediator and Intercessor of believers and the Head of the Church; that He will come to judge the quick and the dead and justly reward the righteous with eternal life and the sinners with everlasting torment.

We believe in the Holy Ghost who is perfect God and the source of all truth, who spoke by the laws, the prophets and the Holy Gospel and who is the champion and Counselor of Christians.

We believe in both the Old and New Testaments, the Holy Scriptures,[2] as the perfect canon of the church, and we believe in all the doctrines, teachings, and mysteries in it, and we earnestly try to live according to all the laws taught to us so that we may stand in the presence of God and men with a good and clean conscience.[3]

We believe that it is the Christ-ordained duty of all true believers to be baptized in the name of the Father, the Son and the Holy Ghost. Also to observe the Holy Communion in remembrance of the life-giving death of our Savior who commanded, "This do in remembrance of me."[4]

1. Translated by the Reverend Edward S. Tovmassian from Stepan Eutudjian, *op. cit.,* pp. 160-162.
2. In Armenian, Holy Scriptures is translated with the word "Asdvadzashoonch" (Breath of God).
3. Acts 24:16.
4. Luke 20:19 (The quotation is erroneous. Should read Luke 22:19).

And if you like to question us further concerning our faith, it is the faith taught in the New Testament.[5] By accepting the Nicene Creed, which is in accordance with the Holy Gospel, we express that we are in unity with the faith of the orthodox church.

And, therefore, we declare and confess that our faith is what the Holy Scriptures have taught, as it should be so, and indeed, how can we accept those requirements which contradict the truth of the Holy Scriptures, and are absolutely forbidden by anathema.[6] Our refusal to accept things that have not been approved by the Holy Scriptures has been construed as rebellion and therefore they have named us as enemies of the church and destroyers of the faith. We deny these accusations, and together, we claim that we love our Nation and the Church so much that we deem it great honor and pride to be called Armenian, as Paul the Apostle declared it about himself.[7]

By nationality we are Armenians, by faith and religion Christian, and we are faithful subjects of the Ottoman Government. Therefore, if in political and religious matters we have made mistakes (we do not consider ourselves infallible), we will accept these mistakes. You know well, however, that the convictions of human nature can only be effected by the evidence of truth and not by coercion, and we cannot work against our consciences, having the fear of God in us.

And now, we implore that this statement of ours be acceptable to your highness, and we hope that you will kindly give us grace and mercy by saving us from these hardships and sufferings.

We remain, most Reverend Lord,
  With good wishes to your highness,

1846, January 22.   Persecuted Christians.

---

5. Rom. 10:17.
6. Gal. 1:8,9.
7. Rom. 9:3.

COMPARISON OF THE THEOLOGICAL POSITIONS OF THE TWO GROUPS

THE NEW CREED

1. Faith alone cannot save a man; but with faith there must be good works.

2. The Church of Christ is the visible "Church Militant" and it has never erred and never can err, and there is no truth of which she is not aware.

3. There are seven sacraments which may not be administered by any private Christian except by men in the Apostolic succession through ordination.

4. Baptism, Confession, and penance are saving ordinances, to be supplemented after death by the mass, alms, and prayers of the church. The unbaptized have no salvation even though they have never sinned.

5. Holy Communion is the true body and blood of Christ.

6. Virginity of Mary is perpetual, crosses and other relics are worthy of adoration, and saints may intercede.

7. Belief in the Church means belief in those things which the Universal Church believes (Which would include creed, traditions, rites, and ceremonies).

THE EVANGELISTIC VIEW

Salvation is by faith alone, justified by the righteousness of Christ, and not by meritorious works, such as prayer, fasting, or penance.

The true Church of Christ is the Invisible Church; the Visible Church can and does err.

There are but two sacraments, Baptism and the Lord's Supper and a Christian duly ordained by a gathered Church may administer them.

Church and-priest craft cannot give salvation, which is obtained by faith; and Baptism does not impute salvation. Man needs the regenerating power of God and the preaching of the Word to be converted.

Holy Communion is the visible symbol of the death of Christ, a perpetual memento of his atoning love and it is not the true body and blood of Christ. A holy life is the true mark of a saved soul. Therefore, it is to be administered to those carefully examined as to their knowledge of the doctrines of the Gospel and their personal piety, and who afford satisfactory evidence.

The veneration of relics, crosses, and pictures, and the practice of praying for the dead, are all contrary to the Scriptures; besides God, no other creature is to be worshipped or adored and Christ is the only Mediator.

Christ is the sole Head of the Church, Savior, Intercessor, and the only Atonement for Sin; believing in the church does not mean believing all the Universal Church believes or the traditions it has received.

142

8. There must needs be gradations in the clergy, the highest having authority to act as viceregent of Christ. Any unworthy cleric does not bring any disgrace upon the creed or status of the church itself.

Any organized group of true Christians is a church of Jesus Christ, and "holiness of life and a conscientious discharge of various duties to God, to our fellow-men, and to ourselves, are not only constantly binding upon all believers, but essential to the Christian character."1

9. Those not believing in the interpretations of the Church of all Christian scripture, rites, and ceremonies—such as Holy Scripture, Holy Spirit, perpetual virginity of Mary as Mother of God, relics of saints, and pictures—must be anathematized.

The Scriptures are the revelation of God's will to man and the sufficient rule of faith and conduct, and the chief instrument appointed by Christ for the conversion of man. Therefore, the Triune God alone is to be worshipped, not the interpretations of the Church.

1. Dwight, *op. cit.*, p. 331.

FIRST ANATHEMA
OF THE PRIEST VERTANES

"From Matteos, the Lord Archbishop and Patriarch of the great metropolitan city of Constantinople, to all our Spiritual Ecclesiastical Officers, and to all of our Armenian Laity, salutation in Jesus Christ.

"The holy apostle Paul, the chosen vessel of the Grace of the Holy Spirit, has well counselled the servants of the Church of God, of every rank and grade, how the clergy especially should stand firm in faith and conversation, with holiness and purity; how the elders and priests, who are ministers of the divine and holy sacraments, should be nourished by the holy faith, and become examples to the faithful in doctrine, life, charity, faith and holiness; not to neglect the grace of God which was given them by the laying on of the hands of the Presbytery; and to take heed to themselves and to their doctrines, so as to both save themselves and those that hear them. All this has the apostle transmitted in writing to Timothy, saying (II, i.6), 'Wherefore I put thee in remembrance that thou stir up the gift of God, which is in thee, by the putting on of my hands. That good thing which was committed to thee, keep by the Holy Ghost which dwelleth in us. Study to show thyself approved unto God, a workman that needeth not to be ashamed, rightly dividing the word of truth. O Timothy, keep that which is committed to thy trust, avoiding profane and vain babblings and oppositions of science falsely so called.'

"But now in these latter times, as according to the inspired prophecy of the apostle, some have departed from the holy faith, and turned aside to the impiety and seduction of devils, speaking falsehood in hypocrisy, deceived by their own consciences and following their sinful lusts, they finally arrive at perdition in newfangled oppositions and errors.

"Of these there is one in our nation, a contemptible wretch, the unworthy priest Vertanes, of Nicomedia. He was some time since ordained over the Church in Nicomedia, by the spiritually illuminated Archbishop Boghos, of that city. This fellow, following his carnal lusts, leaves the Church and his sacred office, and, like a vagabond going about through the metropolis and Nicomedia, babbles out errors, unworthy of his sacred office and dignity, and becomes an occasion of stumbling to many. And altogether throwing aside the holiness of faith, which he had received in the holy and Catholic Armenian Church, he follows the erroneous doctrines of *Modern Sectaries*, and begins to preach their error in Nicomedia, Cesarea, Anatolia, and in Constantinople, and in every place wherever he sets his impious foot, and to overwhelm the simple people in spiritual destruction. After all this, on his return to Constantinople we called him to us kindly, conversed with him many times, beseechingly and mildly, and gave him spiritual counsel necessary and useful to disrobe him of the impiety of his wayward course, and to robe him again in the glorious vestments of the holy and catholic doctrines of the Armenian Church. But he remained obstinately bent upon his wickedness, after the example of Judas, who regarded not the divine command of our Saviour, Jesus, when, in the presence of the other apostles, he said of Judas, 'But woe to that man by whom the Son of man is betrayed; good were it for that man if he had never been born.' To this Judas did not listen, and did not wish ever to think of it, for he did not wish to forsake his wickedness, which he was prepared to do. In like manner this fellow, not wishing to expel the Satanic spirit from himself, and, in order to accomplish his desires, has rejected the holy grace of God, which he received in ordination. He has despised the holy covenant which he covenanted with God, on receiving the holy order of the priesthood. He has denied the Church of Christ which begat him, he has denied the holy laver which received him into sonship to his heavenly Father. And this his impiety he has shown not only by word and deed; but his own manuscript, which we have by us, has vomited out the gall of bitterness which was in his heart.

"And since that deceiver endeavors to creep into houses, and to travel here and there in order to deceive our simple-minded people to the perdition of the soul, therefore hasting to warn my beloved in the faith, I remind you of the apostolical counsel, 'A man that is a heretic after the first and second admonition, reject, knowing that he that is such, is subverted and sinneth, being condemned of himself.' (Tit. iii. 10) For if he that despised Moses' law perished without mercy, of how much sorer punishment do you think him worthy who has despised the immaculate bride of Christ, the holy Church? Behold this man deliberately and wilfully has wandered from the unity of the Church of Christ, an enemy of the *holy Church*, a divider of her members, a cause of scandal, a seducer of the people, a traitor and murderer of Christ, a child of the devil, and an offspring of *Antichrist*, worse than an infidel, or a heathen, since, under the semblance of faith, he teaches the impieties and seductions of *Modern Sectaries*.

"Therefore according to the declaration of our Lord, 'Beware of false prophets, who come to you in sheep's clothing, but inwardly they are ravening wolves, who will not spare the flock,' (Matt. vii. 15), behold this is a ravening and rending wolf, who in sheep's clothing, that is, under the appearance of priestly virtue, comes to you, to rend and devour you, and to lacerate the innocent lambs, the children of our holy Church, with the wicked and hellish teeth of his filthy mouth.

"Wherefore we expel him and forbid him as a Devil, and a child of the Devil, to enter the company of our believers. We cut him off from the priesthood as an amputated member of the spiritual body of Christ, and as a branch cut off from the vine, which is good for nothing but to be cast into the fire. By this admonitory bull, I therefore command and warn my beloved in every city, far and near, not to look upon his face, regarding it as the face of Belial; not to receive him into your holy dwelling, for he is a house-destroying and ravening wolf; not to receive his salutation, but as a soul-destroying and deadly poison; and to beware, with all your households, of the seducing and impious followers of the false doctrine of *Modern Sectaries*; and to pray for them, to the God who remembereth not iniquity, if perchance they may repent, and turn from their wicked paths, and secure the salvation of their souls, through the grace of our Lord and Saviour, Jesus Christ, who is blessed for ever and ever. Amen.

"This bull was written under the shadow of the Cathedral Church of the holy mother of God, at the Patriarchate of all the Armenians, this 12th of January, in the year of our Lord, 1846, Constantinople." [1]

---

1. Berberian, *op. cit.*, pp. 299-303 (for original in Armenian); *Missionary Herald,* June, 1846, pp. 196 f.; Dwight, *op. cit.,* pp. 323f.

SECOND ANATHEMA OF THE ARMENIAN PATRIARCH, ANATHEMATIZING THE WHOLE BODY OF EVANGELICAL ARMENIANS

"Be it known to the pious flock of our Church in the metropolis, that on the last Sabbath, the decree of Anathema was read for the information of the pious, but some of the people understood it as referring only to the cursed nonentity Vertanes, falsely called priest, and not also to the others. Wherefore we considered it necessary to-day to repeat it, and to inform you, that not only that cursed one (Vertanes), but also all that are of his sentiments, deceivers and blasphemers against the Church, and followers of *the corrupt new sect*, are accursed and excommunicated and anathematized, by God, and by all his saints, and by us.

"Wherefore, whoever has a son, that is such an one, or a brother, or a partner (in business), and *gives him bread*, or *assists him in making money*, or *has intercourse with him as a friend*, or *does business with him*—let such persons know that they are nourishing a venomous serpent in their houses, which will one day injure them with its deadly poison, and they will lose their souls. Such persons give bread to Judas. Such persons are enemies of the holy faith of Christianity, and destroyers of the holy Orthodox Church of the Armenians, and a disgrace to the whole nation. Wherefore, *their houses and shops also are accursed*; and *whoever goes to visit them*, we shall learn, and make them public to the holy Church by *terrible* anathemas. For in these days there are some of the poisoned individuals who have become acquainted with their awful error, and having undertaken the necessary penance with repentance, they confess their sin—whom God forgives through the intercession of the holy Church, and our holy Church also receives. On which account we now wait that we may receive all who will return,—and at last, as many souls as remain wicked and hardened, who receiving bodily support or monthly wages, deny their Church, and, like Judas, betray Christ through love of money;—these also, by their names and places, we shall publish to all our churches far and near, with terrible anathema.

"Wherefore by this my letter of notification, I again command and warn the pious to keep aloof from those wicked deceivers;—for the love of the holy faith of Jesus Christ, the glory of the holy Church, and the interest and advantage of your own souls.

"Farewell; and the grace of our Lord Jesus Christ be with you all. Amen."[1]

1. Dwight, *Ibid.*, pp. 326 f.

DECLARATION OF REASONS
FOR ORGANIZING PROTESTANT CHURCHES

"We, Evangelical Christians of the Armenian nation, believing that the true foundation and perfect rule of Christian faith is the Holy Scriptures alone, have cast away from us those human traditions and ceremonies which are opposed to the rules of the Bible, but which our National Church requires. And furthermore, without having had the least intention of separating from it, we have been united together for the special purpose of enlightening and reforming this Church. And since we receive entire the Nicene Creed of the Church, and also since up to the present time no creed embracing particularly these human traditions, has been framed and enjoined upon the members of the Armenian Church as necessary to be received, we could be considered as regular members of the National Church by simply receiving the ancient (Nicene) creed. But in the year 1846, Bishop Matteos, Patriarch of the Armenians, has invented a new creed, embracing particularly these human traditions, and he has insisted upon our accepting and subscribing it.

"But we, obeying God rather than man, have not received it; on account of which he has cast out of the Church, and anathematized us particularly and publicly by name; and, according to his ability, he has also inflicted upon us material injuries. We had indeed, previous to this, suffered persecution of different kinds for our religious opinions; as, for instance, about seven years ago, several of us were sent into exile; and also within about two years, some have been banished, some put in prison, some fined, some bastinadoed, &c.; yet since the present Patriarch rejected us by excommunication from the Church, he has inflicted on us generally various additional bodily penalties. Thus, for several months, all the shops of the Evangelical Armenians were closed; some were unwillingly separated from their homes and parents; and some even from their wives and husbands; bakers and watercarriers were forbidden to bring either bread or water; and to the extent of his ability, he strove, by every species of bodily infliction, to compel us to receive and sign his new confession of faith.

"And although, by the interposed protection of the powerful Ottoman Government, he has been prevented from continuing this severity of persecution, he has to this day, every day on the Sabbath, repeated the command to the Armenian people not to receive us into their houses or shops, or even to look upon us. And, finally, after all these things, he has issued a new bull, and caused it to be read in all the churches on the day of the Catholic Church festival; which bull of excommunication and anathema is also to be read in all the churches throughout the Ottoman Empire, every year successively, at this same festival. Thus he cuts us off, and casts us out for ever from the National Church, by the standing order and high authority of this bull.

"And now it being evident that we cannot be in fellowship with the Armenian Church without receiving human traditions and rites, which, being contrary to the Holy Scriptures, we cannot receive; we, therefore, by the grace and mercy of God, following the doctrine of our Lord Jesus Christ and obeying the Gospel, and consequently being members of his one Catholic and Apostolical Church, do now rightfully and justly constitute ourselves into a Church with the following confession of faith."[1]

1. Eutudjian, *op. cit.*, pp. 169-173.

CONFESSION OF FAITH

1. You believe in the existence of one only living and true God, the Creator, Preserver, and Governor of the universe; omnipotent, omniscient, omnipresent; self-existent, independent, immutable; possessed of infinite benevolence, wisdom, holiness, justice, mercy, and truth, and who is the only proper object of worship.

2. You believe that God exists in three persons, the Father, the Son, and the Holy Ghost; and that these three are one God.

3. You believe that the Scriptures of the old and New Testaments were given by inspiration of God, and are a revelation of his will to man, and the sufficient and only rule of faith and practice.

4. You believe that mankind, in their natural state, are destitute of holiness, and entirely depraved, and justly exposed to the Divine wrath.

5. You believe that the Lord Jesus Christ; perfect God and perfect man, is the only Saviour of sinners, and the only mediator and intercessor between God and man; and that by his perfect obedience, sufferings, and death, he made full atonement for sin, so that all who believe in him will assuredly be saved, and that there is no other sacrifice for sin.

6. You believe that in consequence of the utter wickedness of man, it is necessary that all should be regenerated by the power of the Holy Ghost, in order to be saved.

7. You believe that we are justified by the righteousness of Christ alone, through faith, and not by any fastings, alms, penances, or other deeds of our own; and that while good works are inseparable from true faith, they can never be meritorious ground of salvation before God.

8. You believe that holiness of life, and a conscientious discharge of the various duties we owe to God, to our fellow-men, and to ourselves, are not only constantly binding upon all believers, but essential to the Christian character.

9. You believe that, besides God, no other being is to be worshipped and adored, and that each person in the sacred Trinity is worthy of our worship, which, to be acceptable, must be offered through no other mediation than that of Jesus Christ alone; and that the use of relics, pictures, crosses, and images of any sort, in any act of worship, and of the intercession of saints, is directly contrary to the Scriptures, and highly

displeasing to God; and that prayer of the dead is not authorised in the Word of God.

10. You believe that there will be a resurrection of the dead, both of the just and of the unjust, and a day of judgment; and that the happiness of the righteous, and the punishment of the wicked, commence at death, and continue without end.

11. You believe that any number of believers, duly organized, constitute a church of Christ, of which Christ is the only Head; and that the only sacraments of Christ's Church are *Baptism* and the *Lord's Supper*; the former being the seal of the covenant, and a sign of the purifying operation of the Holy Spirit, and the token of admission into the visible Church; and the latter, in shewing forth by visible symbols the death of Christ, being a perpetual memento of his atoning love, and a pledge of union and communion with him and with all true believers.

12. You believe that the Gospel is the chief instrument appointed by Christ for the conversion of men and for the edification of his people, and that it is the duty of his Church to carry into effect the Saviour's command, "Go ye into all the world, and preach the Gospel to every creature."[1]

---

1. Dwight, *op. cit.*, pp. 336-338; *A.B.C.F.M.*, 1846, pp. 239-240.

WILLIAMS BAY MANIFESTO

"The world is in an age of revolution, a time of changing and becoming. The Church, if it is to be relevant to the world, must speak of God's will in terms of today. Christianity is not a religion for the timid, for it takes courage and strength of conviction to resist that which is comfortable, convenient and traditional in favor of God's will, which may at times be difficult. Christ continually calls His followers to renewal, reform and revolution.

"As the youth of the Armenian Church, we are disturbed by our church's refusal to be a part of the twentieth century, to face the urgent and real problems of today, and to seek Christian solutions to them. Poverty, hunger, disease, wars, racial tensions, social discontent and turmoil sear the world around us, and yet our church concerns itself mainly with erecting costly buildings and monuments and amassing material goods, rationalizing that this is necessary for self-preservation. We want our church to see beyond its own interests, to share others' sufferings and problems.

"At present, in the minds of many Armenians, the Armenian Church's primary function is to act as the defender of nationalism, to protect Armenians from assimilation. This is indicated by their fear of reform, for they worry that with change would come a certain loss of identity. On the contrary, we feel that specific reforms would bring increased dedication and enthusiasm, a renewal and rebirth for our church.

"Apathy and spiritual indifference pervade our church life. Few church members have that sincere relationship with God which is the basis for Christian living. We, as the youth, are not simply condemning the adults of our church; we can see the same problems among ourselves. The ACYOA is suffering from an internal malaise: membership has fallen off, only socials and dances are well attended, spiritual growth has come to a complete standstill.

"The time has come when we, the youth of the Armenian Church, can no longer in conscience allow ourselves to be used as instruments for the preservation of a church which is living in the archaic past. We feel we must make known our discontent with the present antiquated and meaningless structures and institutions and our desire to ameliorate the stagnated condition of the church which is ours. We are told so often that the church belongs to us; therefore we have not only the right but the duty to see that our church relates to the present day and thus becomes meaningful to its members. We are committed to action . . . the watch-word is revolution. Our revolutionary commitment and action addresses itself to a radical concern of making Christ live and grow in our church and members. We are now resolved to speak out and act in accordance with the dictates of our conscience in all areas of life within and without our church, wherever Christ is being crucified anew." [1]

1. *The Armenian Church,* a publication of the Diocese of the Armenian Church of America (New York: November, 1968), Vol. X, No. 6, pp. 1,3.

During the 1968 ACYOA (Armenian Christian Youth Organization of America) General Assembly, convened on Labor Day weekend at Williams Bay, Wisconsin, the youth made this rather unusual statement which was subsequently dubbed the "Williams Bay Manifesto." Seven of the eight Central Council members and twenty-nine of the fifty delegates who said they would proudly affix their signatures to the Manifesto are:

Central Committee Members

(1) Leon M. Hojegian, (2) Ashod R. Aprahamian, (3) Carol Der Boghosian, (4) Nancy C. Kaprelian, (5) Richard Nersigian, (6) Louise K. Yeghissian, (7) Gary Zamanigian.

Official Delegates

(1) Shnork Vartabed Kasparian, (2) Debbie Abdalian, (3) Robert Akulian, (4) Sarkis An-dekian, (5) Joyce Avedisian, (6) Karl Babikian, (7) Ronald Davagian, (8) Vahe H. Derounian, (9) Marcia Gazoorian, (10) John Giragosian, Jr., (11) Father Michael Buttero, (12) Charles Hadjenian, (13) Rosemarie Haigazian, (14) Greg C. Jamian, (15) Steve C. Kaishian, (16) Roseanne Kaprelian, (17) Edward Kargenian, (18) Alan Kazanjian, (19) Albert A. Keshgegian, (20) Flora A. Keshgegian, (21) Father Dajad A. Davidian, (22) Maryann Khachadoorian, (23) George D. Krikorian, (24) Richard Matheossian, (25) Natalia Minasian, (26) Nvart Paparigian, (27) Deirdre Pinzeira, (28) Baykar Tatosian, (29) Toni Vartanian.

BIBLIOGRAPHY

1. General

For awareness of the sociological and anthropological foundations of religious movements:

Reist, Benjamin. *Toward a Theology of Involvement.* Philadelphia: The Westminister Press, 1966.

Troeltsch, Ernest. *The Social Teaching of the Christian Churches.* In Two Volumes. Translated from the German edition of 1911 by Olive Wyon. New York: Harper Torch Books, Harper & Row, 1960.

Wach, Joachim. *Sociology of Religion.* Chicago: The University of Chicago Press, 1944.

Wallace, Anthony F.C. "Revitalization Movements." Wisconsin: George Banta Co. for the American Anthropological Association in the *American Anthropologist* Volume 58, 1956, pp. 264-279.

2. Turkey

For an appreciation of the political and economic, as well as social atmosphere in Turkey in early nineteenth century:

Eversley, Lord and Chirol, Sir Valentine, *Turkish Empire.* London: T. Fisher Unwin, Ltd., 1924 (Fourth Edition).

Gibb, H.A.R. *Mohammedanism.* New York: Oxford University Press, 1962.

Lengyel, Emil. *Turkey.* New York: Random House, 1941.

Luke, Sir Harry. *The Making of Modern Turkey.* London: Macmillan and Co., Ltd., 1936.

Ramsay, W.M. *Impressions of Turkey during Twelve Years' Wanderings.* New York: Putnams, 1897.

Stavrinos, Lefton Stavros. *The Ottoman Empire.* New York: Rinehart & Co., Inc., 1959 (Second printing; first printing, 1957).

Toynbee, Arnold J. and Kirkwood, Kenneth P. *Turkey.* New York: Charles Scribner's Sons, 1927.

Tritton, A.S. *The Caliphs and Their Non-Muslim Subjects.* Oxford: Oxford University Press, 1930.

Vucinich, Wayne S. and Fairchild, Johnson E. "Turkey," *Colliers Encyclopedia,* 1957, Vol. XVIII.

William, John Alden. *Islam.* New York: George Braziller, 1962.

3. The Armenian Evangelicals

For an understanding of the history, movement, aims and problems of the Armenian Evangelicals:

*Adanalian, Garabed. *Houshartzan.* Fresno: Crown Printing Co., 1952.

*Adanalian, Garabed. Unpublished work, preserved in manuscript before his death and now in the hands of his daughter in Washington, D.C.

*Arevelk, The Periodical. Year I, Numbers 10, 13, 16, and 19 January 1884—"The Complaints of the Protestant Armenians against the American Missionaries." Year III, Number 647, March 1, 1886—"Our Protestant Brethren." Year I, Number 28, February 6, 1884—"Missionaries would be respected if they would perform their favors with a humanitarian spirit." (An editorial).

Arpee, Leon. *The Armenian Awakening.* Chicago: The University of Chicago Press, 1909.

Arpee, Leon. *A History of Armenian Christianity.* Princeton: Princeton University Press, 1946. A Centennial Volume Marking the One

*In Armenian.

Hundredth Anniversary of the Armenian Evangelical Movement, sponsored by the Armenian Missionary Association of America, Inc.

Arpee, Leon. *A Century of Armenian Protestantism.* A reprint of five chapters of *The Armenian Awakening* by the Armenian Missionary Association of America, Inc. Princeton: Princeton University Press, 1946.

*Bedikian, A.A. *The Beginning of the Evangelical Movement Among Armenians.* New York: Armenian Missionary Association of America, Inc., 1964.

Bedikian, A.A. *The Rise of the Evangelical Movement Among Armenians.* (English translation of the *Beginning of the Evangelical Movement Among Armenians.*) New York: Armenian Missionary Association of America, Inc., 1970.

Bible Translators, The. April, 1957, p. 76.

Chopourian, Giragos H. *Our Armenian Christian Heritage.* (Armenian Evangelical Union of America, Inc.) Philadelphia: Ideal Press, Inc., 1964.

*Eutudjian, Stepan. *The Rise and Course of Evangelicalism Among Armenians.* Constantinople: Arax Press, 1914.

Goodsell, Fred Field. *Ye Shall Be My Witnesses.* Boston: American Board of Commissioners for Foreign Missions, 1959.

Goodsell, Fred Field. *They Lived Their Faith*—An Almanac of faith, hope, and love. Boston: American Board of Commissioners for Foreign Missions, 1961.

*Googassyantz, H. *Protestantism Among the Armenians of the Caucasus.* Tiflis: Meghoo Hayasdani, 1886.

*Kassouny, Yeghia S. *Loossashavigh* (*The Path of Light: History of the Armenian Evangelical Movement*). Beirut: American Press, 1947.

Kassouny, Yeghia S. *Trail Blazers at Dawn.* Translation of the *Armenian Missionary Spirit in the Armenian Church.* Translated into English by

*In Armenian.

the Armenian Missionary Association of America, Inc. New York (undated).

*Kassouny, Yeghia S. *The Missionary Spirit in the Armenian Church.* Aleppo: Bozolokian Press, 1940.

*Kherlopian, Dicran J. *Vossgemadian* (Golden Anniversary), In Two Volumes. A History of the Armenian Evangelical Movement and the Armenian Evangelical Union of the Near East published on the occasion of the One Hundredth Anniversary of the Movement. Beirut: Armenian Evangelical Union of the Near East, 1950.

*Shmavonian, Arsen. "The Spirit of the Evangelical Church of Armenia." Appearing in *Avedaper,* 1910, pp. 1031 f.

*Yeghiayan, Puzant. *The Why and How of the Separation of the Armenian Denominations.* In Manuscript.

*Yeghiayan, Puzant. *The Separation of the Armenian Catholic and Evangelical Denominations in the Nineteenth Century* (Antelias: Press of the Armenian Catholicate of the See of Cilicia, 1971).

4. The Armenian Apostolic Church

For insights into the workings of the Armenian Apostolic Church and its reasons for withholding support to the American Missionaries and for opposing their Gospel:

Ananikian, M.H. "Armenia (Zoroastrian)." *Encyclopedia of Religion and Ethics.* Vol. X, 1922.

Appleyard, Ernest Silvanus. *Eastern Churches.* London: James Darling, 1850.

Arzoomanian, Zaven. "The Doctrine of the Incarnation according to the 'Scholia de Incarnatione Unigeniti' of Cyril of Alexandria." Philadelphia: A Thesis for the Master of Arts degree at the Department of Religion of Temple University, 1968.

Aslan, K. *Armenia and the Armenians.* New York: Macmillan, 1920.

*In Armenian.

Atamian, Sarkis. *The Armenian Community: The Historic Development of a Social and Ideological Conflict.* New York: Philosophical Library, 1955.

*Berberian, Avedis. *History of Armenians: Beginning with 1772 to 1860.* Constantinople: Boghos Kirishjian and Co. Press, 1871.

Calian, Carnegie Samuel. *Icon and Pulpit.* Philadelphia: The Westminster Press, 1968.

Chakmakjian, Hagop A. *Armenian Christology and Evangelization of Islam.* Leiden: E.J. Brill, 1965.

*Chakmakjian, H.H. *History of Armenia.* Boston: Publication House, 1917, p. 566.

*Chamchean, M. *History of Armenia.* J. Avdall's translation. Calcutta: Bishop's College Press, 1827, Vol. I.

Chamich, Father Michael. *History of Armenia.* Calcutta: Calcutta Bishop's College Press, 1827. In Two Volumes. Abridgement of 3 Volumes of Venice Publication of 1784-86 being the history of Armenia from B.C. 2247 to the year of Christ 1780 or 1229 of the Armenian era, translated from the original by Johannes Avdall, to which is appended a continuation of the history by the translator from 1780 to the present.

Conybeare, Frederick C. *The Key of Truth: A Manual of the Paulician Church of Armenia.* Oxford: Clarendon Press, 1898.

Gregory of Datev. *Books of Questions.* Constantinople, 1729.

*DerMichaelian, Arshak. *Theology of the Armenian Church.* Etchmiadzin: Catholicate, 1911.

*DerMinassian, Y.K. *The Rise and Growth of Medieval Sects.* Yerevan: Armenian Sahka Publication, 1968.

*Der-Movsesian, S. *History of the Armenians: From the Beginning to Our Days.* Highest Course, 2nd ed. revised and completed. In Two Volumes. Venice: St. Lazarre Press, 1922-23.

*In Armenian.

Etmekjian, James. *The French Influence on the Western Armenian Renaissance.* New York: Twayne Publishers, Inc., 1964.

*Guleserian, Papken. *The Reformation of the Armenian Church.* Jerusalem: St. James Press, 1936.

*Hatzooni, V. *Important Problems from the History of the Armenian Church.* Venice: St. Lazarre Press, 1927.

Issaverdens, Rev. James. *The Sacred Rites and Ceremonies of the Armenian Church.* Venice: St. Lazarre Press, 1876.

*Janashian, H. Mesrob V. *History of Contemporary Armenian Literature.* Venice: St. Lazarre Press, 1953.

Lynch, H.F.B. *Armenia: Travels and Studies.* In Two Volumes. London: Longman's Green and Co., 1901.

*Melik-Pakhishian, Sd. D. *The Paulician Movement in Armenia.* Yerevan: University of Yerevan, 1953.

*Mesrob, Kevork. *History of the Armenian Church.* Constantinople: Paros Publishing Co., 1914. In Two Volumes.

*Mesrob, Kevork. Article in *Hairenik Amsakeer* (monthly) 1934, No. 11, p. 95.

*Mesrob, Kevork. *The Entry of Christianity Among the Armenians Before Gregory the Illuminator.* Constantinople: O. Arzooman, 1910, pp. 7-23.

Nersoyan, Tiran. "The Doctrinal Position of the Armenian Church." A Paper Read Before a Circle of Anglican Theologians in Oxford. New York: Diocese of the Armenian Church, 1933.

*Orchanian, K. *History of the Armenian Language and Linguistics.* Marsovan: Nerso and Srabian, 1913, pp. 114-115.

*Ormanian, Malachi. *National History.* In Three Volumes. Constantinople: V. & H. DerNersessian, 1912 (Vol. 1), 1914 (Vol. 2); Jerusalem: Post Mortem Publication Supervised by Archbishop P. Guleserian: St. James Press, 1927.

*In Armenian.

Ormanian, Malachi. *The Church of Armenia.* Translated from the French by Marcar Gregory. London: Nowbray, 1955.

*Paghdikian, Nerses. *The Entry of Protestantism into the World of the Dzopk.* Periodical Agoss, Beirut, Lebanon, 1955 to 1959, Nos. 75, 77, 175, 77-79, 81, 84, 87-88, 90, 100-107, 109-115, 18, 20.

Ricaut, Paul. *The Present State of the Greek and Armenian Churches.* London: John Starkey, 1679.

Sarkissian, Karekin. *The Council of Chalcedon and the Armenian Church.* London: S.P.C.K., 1965.

*Savalanyantz, *History of Jerusalem.* Vol. II. Jerusalem Convent.

Southgate, Horatio. *State of Christianity in Turkey.* New York: Dana and Co., 1856.

5. The Congregational Way

For an understanding of the rise and progress of Congregationalism and its practice in New England out of which the missionaries to Armenians in Istanbul went.

Ahlstrom, Sydney E. *Theology in America.* New York: The Bobbs-Merrill Co., Inc., 1967.

Atkins, G.A. & Tagley, F.L. *History of American Congregationalism.* Boston: Pilgrim Press.

Bennett, John C. *Christians and the State.* New York: Charles Scribner's Sons, 1958.

Church History Magazine—from 1935-1938.

Conn, Howard. *The Dilemma of Congregationalism.* Milwaukee: National Association of Congregational Christian Churches, 1962, p. 6.

Cragg, Gerald R. *From Puritanism to the Age of Reason.* Cambridge: Cambridge University Press, 1950.

*In Armenian.

Cremeans, Charles D. *The Reception of Calvinistic Thought in England.* Urbana: University of Illinois Press, 1949.

Cross, F.L. *The Oxford Dictionary of the Christian Church,* "Paulicians," London: Oxford University Press, 1958, p. 1035.

Davidson, Edward Hutchins. *Jonathan Edwards, the Narrative of a Puritan Mind.* Boston: Houghton Mifflin Co., 1966.

Dexter, Henry Martin. *The Congregationalism of the Last Three Hundred Years.* New York: Harper and Brothers, 1880.

Dexter, Henry Martin. *Congregationalism As Seen In Its Literature.* New York: Harper and Brothers, 1880.

Elwood, Douglas J. *The Philosophical Theology of Jonathan Edwards.* Columbia University Press, 1960. New York.

Ferm, Vergilius. *Puritan Sage: Collected Writings of Jonathan Edwards.* New York: Library Publishers, 1953.

Frank, H. Foster. *A Genetic History of New England Theology.* New York: Russell and Russell, 1963.

Gambrell, May Latimer. *Ministerial Training in Eighteenth Century New England.* New York: Columbia University Press, 1937.

Garrett, Christina. *The Marian Exiles.* Cambridge: Cambridge University Press, 1938. Reprinted 1966.

Grimm, Harold J. *The Reformation Era.* New York: The Macmillan Company, 1961.

Haller, William. *Elizabeth I and the Puritans.* New York: Cornell University Press, 1964.

Haller, William. *The Rise of Puritanism.* New York: Columbia University Press, 1938.

Haroutunian, Joseph. *Piety Versus Moralism.* New York: Henry Holt, 1932.

Heimert, Alan, and Miller, Perry, eds. *The Great Awakening.* American Heritage Series. New York: Bobbs-Merrill Company Inc., 1967.

Hopkins' Works. Boston: Doctrinal Tract & Book Society, 1852. 3 Vols.

Hudson, Winthrop S. *Religion in America.* New York: Scribner, 1965.

Hunter, A.M. *The Teaching of Calvin: A Modern Interpretation.* (2nd Ed. Revised.) London: J. Clarke & Co., 1950.

Jones, R. Tudur. *Congregationalism in England.* London: Independent Press Ltd., 1962.

Knappen, M.M. *Tudor Puritanism.* Chicago: University of Chicago Press, 1939.

Lovett, Richard. *The History of the London Missionary Society, 1795-1895,* Vol. I, p. 49.

McNeill, John Thomas. *The History and Character of Calvinism.* New York: Oxford University Press, 1954.

Mather, Cotton. *Magnalia Christi Americana.* Hartford: Silas Andrus, Roberts & Burr, 1820.

Mead, Sidney Earl. *Nathaniel William Taylor.* Chicago: University of Chicago Press, 1942.

Miller, Perry. *The Life of the Mind in America* (Part I—The Evangelical Basis). New York: Harcourt, Brace and Would, 1965.

Miller, Perry. *Jonathan Edwards.* New Haven: Yale University Press, 1957.

Miller, Perry. *The Marrow of Puritan Divinity.* In Cal. Society of Massachusetts Publications, 1937, Vol. 32.

Miller, Perry. *New England Mind: The Seventeenth Century.* New York: The Macmillan Co., 1939.

Miller, Perry. *Orthodoxy in Massachusetts.* Cambridge: Cambridge University Press, 1933.

Mueller, Wm. A. *The Church and State in Luther and Calvin.* Nashville: Broadman Press, 1954.

Murdock, Kenneth B. *Increase Mather, the Foremost American Puritan.* New York: Russell & Russell, 1953.

Sanders, Thomas G. *Protestant Concepts of Church and State.* New York: Holt, Rinehart and Winston, 1964.

Smith, H. Shelton, Handy, R.T., Loetscher, L.A. *American Christianity.* New York: Charles Scribner's Sons, Vol. I, 1960; Vol. II, 1963.

Smith, Elwyn Allen. *The Presbyterian Ministry in American Culture.* Philadelphia: Westminster Press, 1962.

Spier, J.M. *What is Calvinistic Philosophy?* Translated from the Dutch by Fred H. Klooster, Grand Rapids: W.B. Gerdmans Pub. Co., 1953.

Starkey, Marion L. *The Congregational Way.* New York: Doubleday, 1966.

Stoeffler, F. Ernest. *The Rise of Evangelical Pietism.* Leiden: E.J. Brill, 1965.

Stoeffler, F. Ernest. *Studies in the History of Puritanism.* Leiden: E.J. Brill.

Van Til, Cornelius. *The Case for Calvinism.* Philadelphia: Presbyterian and Reformed Pub., Co., 1964.

Walker, Williston. *A History of the Congregational Churches in the United States.* (In the American Church History Series.) New York: The Christian Literature Co., 1894.

Walker, Williston. *Ten New England Leaders.* New York: Silver, Burdett & Co., 1901.

Walker, Williston. *The Creeds and Platforms of Congregationalism.* Boston: Pilgrim Press, 1960.

Whiting, C.E. *Studies in English Puritanism from the Restoration to the Revolution, 1660-1668.* London: Society for the Propagation of Christian Knowledge, 1931.

Winslow, Ola E. *Jonathan Edwards*. New York: Macmillan, 1940.

6. History of the American Board of Commissioners for Foreign Missions and Their Missionaries to the Armenians.

For an understanding of the history, purposes, methods and operation of the American Board of Commissioners for Foreign Missions and their missionaries for work among Armenians.

American Board of Commissioners for Foreign Missions. "Against the Policy of the American Missionaries Among the Armenian Christians." Boston: A.B.C.F.M., 1867.

—————*American Board.* Boston: A.B.C.F.M., 1914.

—————*Annual Report.* Boston: A.B.C.F.M., 1810-1848, Volumes 1-6.

—————*Avedaper.* Armenian Evangelical Union, 1855-1915.

—————*Condensed Sketch (History), 1810-1885.* Boston: A.B.C.F.M., 1885.

—————*Constantinople Station Centennial: Near East Missions of the American Board.* A.B.C.F.M.: Constantinople, 1931.

—————"Controversy between Missionaries of the A.B.C.F.M. and the Evangelical Armenian Churches in Turkey." New York: A.B.C.F.M., 1882.

—————Correspondence, Minutes, Documents, Letters of the American Board of Commissioners for Foreign Missions housed in the Fulton and Houghton Libraries at Harvard University, Cambridge, Mass.

—————"Duty of American Congregationalists to Foreign Missions." Boston: A.B.C.F.M., 1871.

—————"Duty of American Christians to the Heathen." Boston: A.B.C.F.M., 1866.

————*Haystack Prayer Meeting: One Hundredth Anniversary of the A.B.C.F.M.* Boston: A.B.C.F.M., 1906-1907. Also an account of its origin and spirit.

————*Historical Sketch of the Missions of the A.B.C.F.M. in European Turkey, Asia Minor and Armenia.* Boston: Missionary House, 1866.

————*History of American Missions to the Heathen from Their Commencement to the Present Time.* Compiled chiefly from the published and unpublished documents of the Board by Joseph Tracy. Worcester: Spooner & Howland, 1840.

American Board of Commissioners for Foreign Missions. "Missions to Armenians." (Papers dealing with missions to Armenians, the Armenian controversy and Constantinople mission, located in Houghton Library, Harvard Univ).

————"Mission to Armenians." (Papers dealing with missions to Armenians and the Armenian mission from 1823-1846, located in Houghton Library, Harvard University).

————"Near East Missions." (In Houghton Library, Harvard University, with volumes on "Hints and Cautions," "Near East Letters, 1830-1842," "Near East Material, before 1860," and "Near East Missions, 1860-1900.")

————"Missions to Armenians." (In Houghton Library, Harvard University, with volumes on "Constantinople, 1838-1844." "Constantinople, 1844-1846," and "Armenian Missions, 1846-1859.")

American Board of Commissioners for Foreign Missions. *Missionary Herald* (Variously known or named The Panoplist, The Panoplist and Missionary Herald, and after 1820 as The Missionary Herald). A.B.C.F.M.

————"A Letter from the Missionaries at Constantinople, in Reply to Charges by Rev. Horatio Southgate." Boston: Crocker and Brewster, 1844.

Anderson, Rufus. *History of the Mission of the American Board of Commissioners for Foreign Missions to the Oriental Churches.* Boston: Congregational Publishing Society, 1872. In Two Vols.

Barton, James L. *Daybreak in Turkey.* Boston: The Pilgrim Press, 1908.

Bliss, E.M. *A Concise History of Protestant Missions.* New York: Fleming & Revell Co., 1897.

Chambers, William Nesbit. *Yoljuluk.* London: Simpkin Marshall, Limited, 1928.

Chules, John O., and Smith, Thomas. *The Origin and History of Missions.* Boston: Gould, Kendall & Lincoln, 1837.

Dwight, H.G.O. *Christianity Revived in the Near East.* New York: Baker and Scribner, 1850.

Dwight, H.G.O. *Christianity in Turkey:* A Narrative of the Protestant Reformation in the Armenian Church. (This being a revision of the earlier edition, *Christianity Revived in the Near East.*) London: James Nesbit & Co., 1854.

Hamlin, Cyrus. *My Life and Times Among the Turks.* New York: Carter, 1878.

Goodsell, Fred Field. *They Lived Their Faith.* Boston: American Board of Commissioners for Foreign Missions, 1961.

Hill, Hamilton Andrews. "The American Board: Is Its Proper Relation to the Churches that of Dependence or Domination?" Cambridge: Reprinted from the Andover Review, 1887.

Leonard, D.L. *A Hundred Years of Missions.* 4th edition. New York: Funk and Wagnalls, 1895.

Prime, E.D.G. *Forty Years in the Turkish Empire* (Being Memoirs of Rev. Wm. Goodell). New York: Robert Carter & Bros., 1883.

Richter, Julius. *A History of Protestant Missions in the Near East.* New York: Fleming H. Revell Co., 1910.

Shaw, P.E. *American Contacts with the Eastern Churches, 1820-1870.* Chicago: The American Society of Church History, 1937.

Smith, Eli. *Researches of the Rev. E. Smith and Rev. H.G.O. Dwight in*

Armenia: Including a Journey through Asia Minor, and Into Georgia and Persia, with a Visit to the Nestorian and Chaldean Christians. Boston: Crocker & Brewster, 1833. Two Volumes.

Strong, William Ellsworth. *The Story of the American Board: An Account of the First Hundred Years.* Boston: The Pilgrim Press, 1910.

Scherer, James A. *Missionary, Go Home! A Reappraisal of the Christian World Mission.* Englewood Cliffs, N.J.: Prentice-Hall, 1964.

Spier Collection. Located at Princeton Theological Seminary.

Southgate, Horatio. "Letter to a Friend—Reply to American Board." New York, 1845.

Tracy, Joseph. *History of American Missions to the Heathen from Their Commencement to the Present Time.* Second Edition. New York: M.W. Dodd, 1842.

Tracy, Joseph. *History of the American Board of Commissioners for Foreign Missions* (2nd Edit.). New York: M.W. Dodd, 1842.

United Presbyterian Board. Records of the Mission to Syria (1836-1870). New York: United Pres. Mission Library.